Map of the Netherlands in 1900

Terschelling

WADDEN
SEA

Wierum
Paesens-Moddergat
Oostmahorn
Zoutkamp
Het Bildt/St. Jacobiparochie
Harlingen

Oosterend
Oudeschild

Workum
Hindeloopen

Den Helder
Huisduinen
Wieringen
Stavoren
Lemmer

NORTH SEA

Kolhorn
Petten
Medemblik
Wervershoof
Enkhuizen
Hoorn
Urk
SCHOKLAND
Genemuiden

Egmond aan Zee
ZUIDERZEE

Velsen
IJmuiden
Volendam
Elburg

Marken
Durgerdam/Ransdorp
Harderwijk
IJSSEL

Zandvoort

Noordwijk
Huizen

Katwijk aan Zee
Bunschoten-Spakenburg

Scheveningen

LEK
RIJN

Maassluis
Vlaardingen
Zwartewaal (Brielle)
Charlois
Pernis

WAAL

Goedereede-Havenhoofd
Woudrichem

Ouddorp
Stellendam
MERWEDE

Middelharnis
MAAS

Brouwershaven

Bruinisse
Willemstad

Tholen

Colijnsplaat

GERMANY

Arnemuiden
Yerseke

Breskens

De Paal
Terneuzen

BELGIUM

PLACES WHERE THE FISHERMEN'S GANSEYS HAVE BEEN FOUND ARE MARKED IN RED.

STELLA RUHE

TRADITIONAL DUTCH GANSEYS
FOR CHILDREN

Over 40 sweaters to knit from
30 fishing villages

SEARCH PRESS

CONTENTS

7. MAJOR RIVERS 96

8. WADDEN SEA COAST 104

9. ZUIDERZEE COAST 116

WORD OF THANKS 142

CREDITS 143

KATWIJK, CLASS 5 OF THE STATE SCHOOL, AROUND 1912. MUSEUM KATWIJK

FOREWORD

While researching fishermen's ganseys for *Dutch Traditional Ganseys* and *More Traditional Dutch Ganseys,* I regularly came across photographs showing boys who, from a very young age, were working in the fishing industry and at sea (see chapter 4, 'At Sea'). They wore ganseys like the adult crew – sometimes with clearly different patterns and designs, but quite often theirs were miniature versions.

I was intrigued by the history of these children, especially as even today, in developing countries, an awful lot of young children are being forced to carry out heavy work in appalling conditions – not only on land, in the fishing and shipping industries, in workshops, in retail and industry, but also in prostitution, as child soldiers and as slaves. These days, teenagers in the Netherlands still work hard to be able to afford luxury items. This led me to consider the situation in the nineteenth century, when children had no option but to work to supplement the family income, in order to survive at all. The impact on their health and later life as a result of having to work long hours and do heavy work at such a young age was huge. This situation is now once again in the spotlight, as demonstrated by historical television programmes such as *The Children Who Built Victorian Britain*.

The history of the ganseys, the fishing industry and the social and cultural conditions they came from, are described in detail in *Dutch Traditional Ganseys* and *More Traditional Dutch Ganseys*. In these books, I discussed the origin and use of the ganseys, the rapid developments in fishing during the second half of the nineteenth century, life on board a herring lugger and the living conditions of fishermen and their families, as the ganseys cannot be separated from these subjects. There are many stories and anecdotes about the fishing life in that time, which I have included in those books and here, as they give such a beautiful portrait of an era.

This book focuses on child labour in the fishing industry. I heard and read touching stories about boys who often had to go fishing at a very young age, some as young as seven or eight, and many by the age of eleven or twelve, and who were given the most terrible jobs on board. The chapter 'Child Labour and Compulsory Education'

(see chapter 2) focuses on the way people thought about children and child labour in general and in the fishing industry in particular around 1900. Sometimes, the information in this book differs from the first two books, as a result of new data and progressive insight.

A number of the ganseys in this book are based on old photographs that are included in the first two books, but the children's ganseys were neither discussed nor charted out. Recent finds, including photographs of primary school classes from fishing villages from around 1900, have been added. In my search for lost ganseys as a whole, I have so far been able to distinguish more than 160 unique ganseys from nearly sixty towns, which have been published in these three books.

The ganseys can be knitted by studying the charts and design sketches, all using the simple T-model, which was at the time, and still is, used for sweaters. The sizes run from twelve months to approximately fourteen years old, but can easily be adjusted to any child's size if you use the chest width and the instructions in chapter 5, 'Knitting', and follow the general knitting instructions for ganseys, so that you know exactly what to do and how. The model of a gansey is always the same, which is why I give general instructions on the basis of which you can knit any gansey, with the calculations based on your swatch. If you have little experience knitting sweaters, it is best not to start with the most complicated pattern, but with a simple one to get the hang of it. The ganseys in this book are knitted in the original colour palette, but you are of course free to choose the colours you want.

We did not find pictures with children in ganseys in all towns in *Dutch Traditional Ganseys* and *More Traditional Dutch Ganseys*, so some towns are missing from this book. Of course, you can knit a children's gansey using a chart from one of the first two books and the size table from this book. It is important to use durable, good wool or – if you think you are going to wash the gansey very often or if it is meant for a small child – a good quality wool/acrylic, cotton or cotton/acrylic yarn.

Stella Ruhe
Amsterdam, 2016

PART OF AN UNKNOWN STEAM LUGGER WITH CREW, INCLUDING A REMARKABLY LARGE NUMBER OF YOUNG
BOYS, POSSIBLY THE CREW OF TWO OR MORE SHIPS, CA. 1906. VLAARDINGEN CITY ARCHIVES

1 THE GANSEY

Terschelling

WADDEN
SEA

Wierum
Paesens-Moddergat
Oostmahorn
Zoutkamp

Het Bildt/St. Jacobiparochie

Harlingen

Oosterend

Oudeschild

Workum

Hindeloopen

Den Helder
Huisduinen

Wieringen

Stavoren
Lemmer

NORTH SEA

Kolhorn

Petten

Medemblik

Wervershoof
Enkhuizen

Hoorn

Urk
SCHOKLAND

Genemuiden

Egmond aan Zee

ZUIDERZEE

Volendam

Elburg

Velsen
IJmuiden

Marken

Durgerdam/Ransdorp

IJSSEL

Zandvoort

Harderwijk

Noordwijk

Huizen

Katwijk aan Zee

Bunschoten-Spakenburg

Scheveningen

LEK
RIJN

Maassluis
Vlaardingen
Zwartewaal (Brielle)
Charlois
Pernis

WAAL
Woudrichem

Goedereede-Havenhoofd
Ouddorp
Stellendam
Middelharnis

MERWEDE

MAAS

Brouwershaven

Bruinisse
Tholen
Willemstad

Colijnsplaat

GERMANY

Arnemuiden
Yerseke

Breskens
De Paal
Terneuzen

BELGIUM

PLACES WHERE THE FISHERMEN'S GANSEYS HAVE BEEN FOUND ARE MARKED IN RED.

STELLA RUHE

TRADITIONAL
DUTCH GANSEYS
FOR CHILDREN

Over 40 sweaters to knit from
30 fishing villages

SEARCH PRESS

CONTENTS

7. MAJOR RIVERS 96

8. WADDEN SEA COAST 104

9. ZUIDERZEE COAST 116

WORD OF THANKS 142

CREDITS 143

KATWIJK, CLASS 5 OF THE STATE SCHOOL, AROUND 1912. MUSEUM KATWIJK

FOREWORD

While researching fishermen's ganseys for *Dutch Traditional Ganseys* and *More Traditional Dutch Ganseys,* I regularly came across photographs showing boys who, from a very young age, were working in the fishing industry and at sea (see chapter 4, 'At Sea'). They wore ganseys like the adult crew – sometimes with clearly different patterns and designs, but quite often theirs were miniature versions.

I was intrigued by the history of these children, especially as even today, in developing countries, an awful lot of young children are being forced to carry out heavy work in appalling conditions – not only on land, in the fishing and shipping industries, in workshops, in retail and industry, but also in prostitution, as child soldiers and as slaves. These days, teenagers in the Netherlands still work hard to be able to afford luxury items. This led me to consider the situation in the nineteenth century, when children had no option but to work to supplement the family income, in order to survive at all. The impact on their health and later life as a result of having to work long hours and do heavy work at such a young age was huge. This situation is now once again in the spotlight, as demonstrated by historical television programmes such as *The Children Who Built Victorian Britain*.

The history of the ganseys, the fishing industry and the social and cultural conditions they came from, are described in detail in *Dutch Traditional Ganseys* and *More Traditional Dutch Ganseys*. In these books, I discussed the origin and use of the ganseys, the rapid developments in fishing during the second half of the nineteenth century, life on board a herring lugger and the living conditions of fishermen and their families, as the ganseys cannot be separated from these subjects. There are many stories and anecdotes about the fishing life in that time, which I have included in those books and here, as they give such a beautiful portrait of an era.

This book focuses on child labour in the fishing industry. I heard and read touching stories about boys who often had to go fishing at a very young age, some as young as seven or eight, and many by the age of eleven or twelve, and who were given the most terrible jobs on board. The chapter 'Child Labour and Compulsory Education'

(see chapter 2) focuses on the way people thought about children and child labour in general and in the fishing industry in particular around 1900. Sometimes, the information in this book differs from the first two books, as a result of new data and progressive insight.

A number of the ganseys in this book are based on old photographs that are included in the first two books, but the children's ganseys were neither discussed nor charted out. Recent finds, including photographs of primary school classes from fishing villages from around 1900, have been added. In my search for lost ganseys as a whole, I have so far been able to distinguish more than 160 unique ganseys from nearly sixty towns, which have been published in these three books.

The ganseys can be knitted by studying the charts and design sketches, all using the simple T-model, which was at the time, and still is, used for sweaters. The sizes run from twelve months to approximately fourteen years old, but can easily be adjusted to any child's size if you use the chest width and the instructions in chapter 5, 'Knitting', and follow the general knitting instructions for ganseys, so that you know exactly what to do and how. The model of a gansey is always the same, which is why I give general instructions on the basis of which you can knit any gansey, with the calculations based on your swatch. If you have little experience knitting sweaters, it is best not to start with the most complicated pattern, but with a simple one to get the hang of it. The ganseys in this book are knitted in the original colour palette, but you are of course free to choose the colours you want.

We did not find pictures with children in ganseys in all towns in *Dutch Traditional Ganseys* and *More Traditional Dutch Ganseys*, so some towns are missing from this book. Of course, you can knit a children's gansey using a chart from one of the first two books and the size table from this book. It is important to use durable, good wool or – if you think you are going to wash the gansey very often or if it is meant for a small child – a good quality wool/acrylic, cotton or cotton/acrylic yarn.

Stella Ruhe
Amsterdam, 2016

PART OF AN UNKNOWN STEAM LUGGER WITH CREW, INCLUDING A REMARKABLY LARGE NUMBER OF YOUNG
BOYS, POSSIBLY THE CREW OF TWO OR MORE SHIPS, CA. 1906. VLAARDINGEN CITY ARCHIVES

1 THE GANSEY

Ganseys were worn as work wear and outerwear by fishermen from Dutch fishing villages on the coasts, along the major rivers and inland waterways between approximately 1860 and 1950. The oldest photograph of a Dutch fisherman wearing a gansey dates from 1867/68. The man in the photograph – taken in a studio in the coastal town of Sunderland in the county of Tyne & Wear on the northeast coast of England – is a Jan Storm from Vlaardingen. He was brought ashore after having survived the sinking of the hooker *Haringvisscherij* VN 62. The photograph is a very recent find (2016), donated to Vlaardingen Museum (fig. 1). The gansey has an unknown pattern with horizontal strips separated by garter stitch ridges as seen in other ganseys from Vlaardingen. The motif looks a bit like the bramble gansey of Noordwijk, but it could also be a double moss stitch.

It is possible that the ganseys were worn as outerwear around 1840–50, but we have not found any pictures or photographs from that time.

This in itself is not strange: photography was invented in the first half of the nineteenth century and having your picture taken was very expensive at that time. Almost nowhere were ganseys included in clothing lists for fishermen who went to sea, while all the other clothing was mentioned in detail. This is probably one of the reasons why people in most fishing villages no longer had any knowledge

of the ganseys, and usually vehemently denied that they had been worn at all: as well as the fact that

1 PORTRAIT OF SAILOR-FISHERMAN JAN STORM (TWENTY-TWO YEARS OLD) WITH AN OCTANT IN HIS HAND AND HIS SOU'WESTER ON THE TABLE, SURVIVOR OF THE SHIPWRECK WITH THE VLAARDINGSE HOOKER *HARINGVISSCHERIJ* VN 62, MADE IN A STUDIO IN SUNDERLAND, ENGLAND, DECEMBER 1867. COLLODION SILVER PRINT TECHNIQUE. VLAARDINGEN MUSEUM, DONATED BY REINDER STORM, IMAGE PROCESSED BY JAN OVERDUIN

knitting was 'just' women's work, ganseys were work clothes that would be left to wear out. As my research has shown, the women, mothers, sisters and daughters often did knit these ganseys.

ORIGIN

Ironically, the ganseys have their origins in the sweaters knitted by men as export products on the Channel Islands of Guernsey and Jersey since the sixteenth century (fig. 2). They found their way north via the English south, east and west coasts, where fishermen started wearing the ganseys on

2 GANSEY FROM GUERNSEY, STELLA RUHE, AMSTERDAM

board the ships around 1825–1830 as work and outerwear. In terms of design and motifs, these ganseys still looked very similar to the linen smocks – shirts made using the smocking technique – that had previously been worn as outerwear. In those regions, the ganseys were called smock, guernsey, gansey or frock (fig. 3). In the second half of the

nineteenth century, the patterns disseminated from the north in Scotland to the south via the so-called 'herring girls', who were usually Scottish women and girls who gutted herring and followed the fleet south by train during the herring season. While they were waiting for the fish, they would knit. The lanolin in the wool was soothing for their

3A KNITTING HERRING GIRLS, ENGLAND, CA. 1910

hands, sore and injured from working with knives and salt all day (fig. 3a). In English coastal towns, people looked forward to the arrival of the herring girls, to see which patterns they were knitting.

The dissemination of ganseys has everything to do with herring. As the Dutch fished for herring in the North Sea, the international waters off the east coast of England (a skill the Dutch mastered in the thirteenth to fourteenth centuries), they came into regular contact with English and Scottish fishermen. Many fishermen from Dutch coastal towns switched to lucrative herring after the lifting of the gutting ban in 1857, which allowed vessels from ports other than Vlaardingen and Maassluis to fish for herring (see gutting ban box, page 23). The Dutch fishermen took to wearing the practical and warm sweaters as outerwear, after having worn them as underwear previously. They would trade tea, tobacco and Dutch gin (*jenever*) for sweaters, socks, mittens and hats on the Shetland Islands, which was their base for fishing in early June when the herring migration started, and take the garments home with them (fig. 4), despite the import ban on wool and wool products. Another example of this trade is the *Itse* hat, worn by men on the Dutch

3 BOY BAND FROM POLPERRO, CORNWALL, ENGLAND, CA. 1885

island of Marken (fig. 5). They called Shetland *Hitland*, and the men from Marken, sailing on the herring luggers from Vlaardingen and IJmuiden, were so taken by the colourful knitted fabrics that they started wearing them at home, in addition to stockings and mittens from the Shetland Islands. The fishermen also regularly visited the towns

4 DUTCH BOYS FROM SCHEVENINGEN IN LERWICK, SHETLAND ISLANDS, CA. 1900. SHETLAND MUSEUM & ARCHIVES

along the English east coast to take in fresh water and salt for gutting.

Since many fishermen from all over the country signed on to lugger fleets in the large port of Vlaardingen and from Katwijk and Scheveningen, the custom of wearing ganseys as outerwear quickly spread to all fishing villages (smaller towns and villages did not have their own ports and could not land their keel luggers on the beach in the same way as the flat-bottomed *bomschuiten* they used before). In 1905, the Vlaardingen fishing fleet alone comprised 2,380 men, approximately fourteen men per lugger. Of these fishermen, 1,137 were from Vlaardingen. The other crew members came from ninety-one different towns all over the Netherlands! That's why crew photographs show ganseys from various towns and cities, which initially made it difficult to determine the origin of the ganseys. When the dominant position of Vlaardingen within the herring fishery became clear (see gutting ban box, page 23), this became much simpler.

Many fishermen wore machine-knitted sweaters, smooth stocking (stockinette) stitch with an eye of God on the chest, which were made in England

for the Dutch market. These were worn as status symbols, because if you could buy a gansey as a fisherman – who were usually poor – it showed you had some money. These ganseys were first worn as Sunday best, and then later as work wear. A gansey like this would last up to ten years.

KNITTING

The ganseys evolved based on the local knitting traditions. Women would expand their library of patterns and symbolic motifs (see pages 48–50), knitting the T-model ganseys, the traditional shape up to approximately 1930, knitted as a tube in the round, in knit, purl and cable stitches known by heart and all handed down from mother to daughter. The ganseys were knitted on thin needles, to make them as windproof and waterproof as possible. In the cold, out at sea, but also in the damp, draughty houses, wool sweaters were ideal for giving warmth, as apart from a small stove in the forecastle, kitchen or living room, ships and houses had no other sources of heating.

Until about 1930, fishermen were the only people who wore ganseys as outerwear. In the mid-1920s, Coco Chanel introduced sweaters as fashion, inspired by the Breton ganseys. From that time on, tailoring techniques and written patterns were introduced for knit sweaters. Fisherwomen used sagathy (see page 44), a type of yarn spun from the belly wool of the native Texelaar sheep, in blue, natural, grey and black. Sagathy was manufactured in Veenendaal, Leiden and in the province of Brabant until after the Second World War. As other, softer wool types became available, sagathy was used less and less, as people felt it was too coarse. Its manufacture was discontinued in 1960.

5 *ITSE* HAT, KNITTED ON THE SHETLAND ISLANDS, BROUGHT BACK TO THE NETHERLANDS BY FISHERMEN FROM MARKEN. DUTCH OPEN AIR MUSEUM, ARNHEM

6 GANSEY FROM PERNIS, CA. 1900. VLAARDINGEN CITY ARCHIVES
7 GANSEY FROM ZWARTEWAAL, CA. 1900. VLAARDINGEN CITY ARCHIVES
8 GANSEY FROM VLAARDINGEN, CA. 1905. DUTCH OPEN AIR MUSEUM, ARNHEM
9 GANSEY FROM ENKHUIZEN, CA. 1900. GWEN SEBUS
10 GANSEY FROM KATWIJK, CA. 1910. KATWIJKS MUSEUM
11 GANSEY FROM WERVERSHOOF, CA. 1955. OUD WERVERSHOOF
12 PIETER JOHANNES VAN DER MOLEN, FROM ENKHUIZEN, CA. 1935. ZUIDERZEE MUSEUM, ENKHUIZEN

DESIGNS AND DATING

The designs used help date the ganseys; the oldest ganseys originate from Pernis and Zwartewaal (fig. 6, 7). The fishermen from these towns were the first to come into contact with English and Scottish fishermen when fishing for cod and haddock in the Arctic Ocean. The design of these ganseys, with a pronounced yoke and motifs in horizontal bands, clearly shows that they are inspired by smocked shirts, which were also part of the usual fishing attire in these towns. Later, the ganseys from, for example, Vlaardingen, lost this yoke shape, but they did retain the horizontal bands (fig. 8). Some time later, a vertical central band was introduced, as in the Enkhuizen gansey (fig. 9), or motifs in vertical bands, as in the Katwijk gansey (fig. 10). More recent ganseys have one continuous motif (fig. 11) and after 1930, designs were inspired by fashion sweaters (fig. 12).

WORK WEAR

On board, ganseys were worn day and night. Fishermen worked four-hour shifts, followed by four hours off, and could be called back on deck at any time if the weather changed. They kept their clothes on when they turned in. The ganseys would get dirty and greasy, which made them more windproof and waterproof. The fishermen would not wash (either themselves or their clothes), because the fresh water on board was only to be used for tea, coffee and cooking. And they wouldn't use salt water to clean themselves – only the ship was cleaned that way. Because salt water causes nasty wounds, the fishermen often wore a handkerchief or scarf around their neck. On the ship, they would wear boots, which were replaced by clogs when they got to shore. Clogs were warmer than boots, but were slippery on deck. This could be dangerous, more so because most fishermen could not swim; however, if you went overboard on the open sea, being able to swim was of no use to you anyway.

Hardly any original ganseys have survived. The ganseys held in a few museum collections are all of a more recent date,

13 ORIGINAL GANSEY FROM HARDERWIJK, CA. 1925 MARIANNE EISMA, AMSTERDAM
14 ORIGINAL GANSEY FROM SCHEVENINGEN, CA. 1935. MUZEE SCHEVENINGEN
15 ORIGINAL GANSEY FROM SCHEVENINGEN, CA. 1950. MUZEE SCHEVENINGEN

usually from the 1930s, 1940s and 1950s (fig. 13, 14, 15). As they were work wear, they were worn until they fell to pieces. Photographs are now the only source for older ganseys. The photos taken around 1900 were made using the glass plate method, which gives much sharper pictures, so the patterns can be seen really well.

PRACTICAL SWEATERS

Everything about the ganseys was practical:
• They had no seams, so they didn't give wind or water a chance: the ganseys were knit in the round and the shoulder seams were closed with a knit cast-off. For ganseys, you were not allowed to use a needle and thread for religious reasons, as Jesus' shirt had no seams either.
• The ganseys had a T-model, making it easy to hang them up on a long stick through the sleeves to dry them when they got wet.
• They had little ease (chest + 3–6cm/1¼–2¼in) and were tightly knitted on much thinner needles than we would use today, to make them windproof. Sometimes, one shoulder would be left open, fastened with buttons (fig. 16) or they would have a front placket (fig. 17) to make it easier to pull over the head. Because of the densely knitted fabric, the ganseys required a lot of yarn, sometimes more than a kilo, making them relatively heavy. The sleeves were on the short side to keep the hands

and forearms free while working. Often, sleeve protectors were worn, made from leather or oiled cotton. Fishermen often had very nasty wounds called *mouwvreters* ('sleeve rippers'), from the cuffs to their fingers, because they held their arms and hands in salt water while gutting herring (see box, page 23) with razor-sharp knives, or from being injured by the hooks of the longliners (see page 24). Not everyone had the money to buy good waterproof gloves.
• The vulnerable cuffs, which wore a lot faster, were sometimes knitted with the yarn held double.
• The turned cuffs visible on many photos were not just simply made by knitting in the same thickness as the rest of the sweater. They were also a fashion phenomenon and very practical; they were used to keep cigars, which were considered to be healthy in those days, and boys would smoke from a young age.
• Elastic had not been invented yet. With time, the collar would become loose and start to sag and let cold and water in. For that reason, a cord was pulled through holes along the neckline, with tassels or pompoms at the ends, to close the sweater tightly around the neck (fig. 18). The tassels had another function: when shaking or beating the herring out of the nets, the by-catch would also come out, including jellyfish spraying their poison, which sometimes ended up in the eyes. Fishermen could

YOUNG FISHERMAN, POSSIBLY FROM WIERUM. IES MUSEUM

17 JOHANNIS VAN DONGEN FROM MIDDELHARNIS. VAN DONGEN FAMILY COLLECTION

18 YOUNG FISHERMAN FROM VLAARDINGEN. VLAARDINGEN MUSEUM

use the tassels to wipe the poison from their eyes. The cords were common in Dutch ganseys. A few rows before casting off the neckline, a row of holes would be knitted. I have also seen ganseys with the cord simply inserted through the ribbed collar (fig. 14, page 10).

• The ganseys were rarely washed, and often never taken off during a fishing trip. The herring were caught at night or early in the morning, when they would swim to the surface. As a result, the ganseys were very dirty and greasy, but this had the advantage that it made them water- and windproof. It also had negative consequences: fishermen were sometimes so dirty that the clothing fused to the skin. If they had to go to hospital, they were first soaked in oil for two days to pull off the clothing. They would then be scrubbed down with lots of soap, and sometimes they died within days, as their skin had lost its protective layer.

• If the fishermen were very poor, which was the rule rather than the exception, the ganseys would be knit in stocking (stockinette) stitch for the largest part, from the bottom hem to the chest and the sleeves, with motifs only for the part that had to stay extra warm: the chest and lungs. This applied to both the front and back. Knitting a motif took more yarn than stockinette, and was therefore also warmer.

• In contrast to the Scottish and English sweaters, only the very oldest ganseys had gussets for the armpits and neck (fig. 19, 20). In later ganseys, the gussets have disappeared. The gussets were knitted to give the neckline more shape, and bound off straight on both front and back. This meant it didn't matter which way was front or back, making it easy to pull them on quickly. The armpit gussets would allow for a bit more space to move.

• The ganseys were forever patched up and reknitted. The cuffs and elbows would wear first. Because the sleeves were knitted down from the armhole, it was relatively easy to partly rip out the sleeves and reknit them. Ganseys often had smooth sleeves or a motif above the elbows. If the elbows were worn, ripping out would have no effect on the motif. Often, the yarn initially used was no longer available and the knitter would simply use whatever yarn they had at hand. If the gansey could no longer be patched up and was totally worn and threadbare, it would be used as a deck mop or polishing rag.

• It is said that in some towns, such as Bunschoten-Spakenburg, Elburg and Urk, the ganseys would be knitted bigger than the size intended, and then felted in hot water, to make them even more waterproof and windproof. The disadvantage was that the fabric could not be ripped back and reknitted if the sweater had holes. However, no photos have been found to prove this method was in use.

19 ARMPIT GUSSET

20 NECK GUSSET

MYTHS

There are many myths surrounding the fishermen and their ganseys. One is that each fishing village had its own gansey. This is only partly true; only very close-knit and 'insular' communities developed their own gansey; most women simply looked at each other's work andwould knit their own variations. In most towns, I came across various, very different ganseys; women had their own preferences when it came to knitting patterns, and what was in fashion also played a role, as they do now.

Another myth is that all ganseys were blue. We don't have any colour photographs of these ganseys, but photos from, for example, Den Helder (page 56) also show cream-coloured ganseys, while in Volendam people would wear black ganseys. In addition, grey ganseys have been found, and numerous shades of blue were worn.

It was said that women knitting ganseys for their fiancés would knit in some of their own hair as a token of love and for symbolic protection. Even though this may have been the case, no such ganseys have been found anywhere.

BOYS AND GIRLS

The old photographs show a lot of boys wore ganseys just like the adults. These boys were often deployed as the youngest crew members on herring boats. On a school photograph from Katwijk, I also discovered a couple of girls wearing ganseys. It is possible that these were knitted for their brothers and were passed on, as generally girls did not wear ganseys at that time.

GIRL WEARING A GANSEY; DETAIL FROM FIG. 21 BELOW.

21 CLASS 2 OF THE ORPHANAGE STREET KINDERGARTEN, KATWIJK ANN ZEE, CA. 1924. KATWIJKS MUSEUM

CLASS 4 OF THE STATE PRIMARY SCHOOL IN KATWIJK,
CA. 1910. KATWIJKS MUSEUM

2 CHILD LABOUR AND COMPULSORY EDUCATION

For us, it is incomprehensible that children between the ages of eight and ten would work twelve hours a day in a factory, six or seven days a week, even working night shifts; we would call it inhumane. But in the nineteenth century this was quite common, as is still often the case in developing countries. Child labour occurred in all sectors: agriculture, fishing, shipping, mining, heavy industry, workshops and shops. There was no compulsory education yet; you would learn a trade on the job, if there was no money to pay for school. Children would almost always do the same job as their parents – from cradle to grave. Children also needed to work to supplement the family income, because the parents alone would not earn enough to support a large family.

There were no contraceptives, no pensions, so having many children was a way to make sure you were cared for when you got old. This had been the 'system' for centuries, and everyone considered it to be normal. Hard work and the odd beating were part of growing up. People did not recognize that this was one of the reasons why children died prematurely, in addition to what we now consider to be easily curable diseases, lack of sanitation and

hygiene, poor drinking water, poor housing and much more. Child mortality was considered to be a fact of life. With many children in such poor conditions, only the strongest survived.

INDUSTRIAL REVOLUTION

The mid-nineteenth century saw industrialization in Europe and also in the Netherlands. The world population had grown to about 1 billion (almost 8 billion now), and the Netherlands had a population of 4.5 million (now 17 million). During the industrial revolution in the nineteenth century, one factory after another was built. The textile and pottery industries were booming, as well as the fisheries, which saw the introduction of faster vessels (luggers and sloops) and better cotton nets (made more sturdy by tanning them in boilers with oak bark), which made it possible to catch more fish. All over Europe, major exhibitions were held showcasing the latest developments and inventions (see box, page 16). Enterprising ship owners, such as A.E. Maas from Scheveningen, who visited one of the large fishery exhibitions held at the time, introduced the much faster *lougre*, a sailing lugger, and the *chalouppe*, the sloop, which gradually

The Hague to allow children to work as much as possible. For employers, child labour was particularly lucrative. Children would work long hours, because the more they produced, the more they got paid. Factory owners paid very low wages and children had to do what they were

23 WORKERS, INCLUDING CHILDREN, IN A BRICK AND ROOF TILE FACTORY

replaced the slow herring busses, hookers and flat-bottomed *bomschuiten*. Cotton nets replaced the heavy, unwieldy hemp nets. Children, both boys and girls (the latter not on ships but in the fish factories), were put to work everywhere, especially as their small fingers could fit in dangerous places adult fingers could not get to.

Factory owners were in dire need of this cheap labour force. They lobbied the government in

International Fisheries Exhibition in London, 1883
The following special promotion not only shows that children had to work hard, but that sometimes fun things happened as well.

On 19 May 1883, the International Fisheries Exhibition opened in South Kensington, London, where the Netherlands also had a major presence. In order to make a good impression, the Seafishing College had invited girls from eight fishing villages to join the Dutch delegation wearing traditional dress: the forerunners of the Volendam cheese girl and Frau Antje, characters which came to epitomize Dutchness. After the committee gave assurances that the girls would be well looked after, the parents of girls from five fishing villages gave their permission: Harderwijk (Mekje Petersen), Paesens-Moddergat (Trijntje Visser, whose father had just died in March, during the major fishing disaster, see Dutch Traditional Ganseys, page 126), Scheveningen, Spakenburg and Zandvoort (Maartje Z.). The parents of the girls from Arnemuiden, Marken

and Urk did not give permission for the girls to travel. On 13 May, the girls were received at the palace of the Prince and Princess of Wales: Albert Edward — later King Edward VII (the eldest son of Queen Victoria And Prince Albert) — and his wife Alexandra. They got to play with the young princes and princesses. The girls only had to be at the exhibition for two hours and also visited cultural sights and theatres. The next day, photographs were taken and sketches made for various newspapers, including The Graphic *(fig. 24 and 25). When they left for Harwich by train on 16 May, the platform was teeming with curious people, who feasted their eyes on the girls, but never committed 'any rudenesses'.*

Jan P. van de Voort,
Vlaardingen Museum

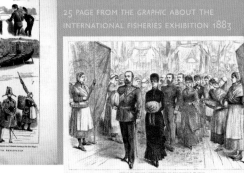

told. Sometimes they had to work up to fourteen hours, from five o'clock in the morning to seven o'clock in the evening or even later, under appalling conditions. The situation was especially appalling in the textile industry (fig. 22), in rope yards/walks, glassworks and pottery factories (fig. 23). There were no rules and regulations regarding working hours and conditions, and both boys and girls worked in shifts and operated dangerous machines or worked near hot ovens. They often went to work sick, poorly fed and dressed, and still tired after only a few hours' sleep, which resulted in many – regularly fatal – accidents. Children would also simply die of exhaustion.

PROTESTS

Around 1860 it was mainly doctors and teachers who protested against the terrible working conditions in the factories and workshops and on board ships. They felt that children should be at least twelve before starting work and should first complete primary school. They saw on a daily basis how unhealthy it was to have to work so hard and such long hours at such a young age. The children were lagging far behind in their physical and mental development, and as a result many boys were declared unfit for military service. Boys of eighteen years of age had the body of a nine-year-old. The average worker would not live past the age of thirty-two. There was also a fear that girls who had to work in the factories would not learn the skills to become good mothers.

In 1863, the writer Jacob Jan Cremer visited a textile factory in Leiden and was appalled by what he saw. He described the terrible working conditions in his novella, *Factory Children: A plea, but not for money* (*Fabriekskinderen. Een bede, doch niet om geld*), in which he also appealed to King William III to intervene. Cremer gave lectures throughout the country and his audience was equally indignant. But even then, politics reacted far too slowly. In 1870, in the newspaper *Het Vaderland*, he wrote 'A word to his countrymen', calling them to send a barrage of petitions to the government. When it became clear how much support he had, he published a 'Public Letter to His Excellency the Minister of Home Affairs', also in *Het Vaderland*. At long last, something changed in the way the public thought about child labour.

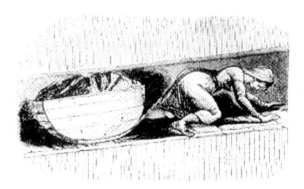

26 CHILD WORKING IN A MINE SHAFT, ENGLAND

CHILD PROTECTION LAWS

The Netherlands does not have a very good reputation when it comes to adapting to and thinking about changing circumstances: not only was it one of the last nations to abolish slavery, it was also the last European country to end child labour. Earning money and potential costs were always more important. Around 1863, countless children from poor families were still working.

The first child protection law in the Netherlands, *Loi concernant les Mines, les Minières et les Carrières*, or the 1810 Mining Act, was introduced by Emperor Napoleon on 21 April 1810, by means of an imperial decree (at that time, the Netherlands was under French rule): children under the age of ten were not allowed to work in the mines (fig. 26).

It was not until 1874, sixty-four years later, that left-liberal MP Samuel van Houten submitted a bill prohibiting child labour before the age of twelve: The Law on Measures to Combat Excessive Labour and Neglect of Children. This was 'not applicable to domestic and personal services and to field work', but mainly to factories and workshops (fig. 27). Van Houten's law was passed, but because it was not enforced the law was constantly broken in the first few years.

27 LIBERAL MP SAMUEL VAN HOUTEN

In 1887, the Dutch Lower House conducted a parliamentary inquiry into working conditions in factories and workshops and on ships, in order to determine whether the 1874 act was being complied with and whether child labour was a thing of the past. The inquiry proved the opposite and resulted in the introduction of new laws which gradually drove back child labour. The 1889 Factory Acts prohibited children under the age of twelve from working, including in agriculture, and contained a number of rules to limit the working hours of children under the age of sixteen. Inspectors were appointed to enforce compliance with the law. Ship owners, in particular, protested against these new laws, bringing up all kinds of false arguments, such as that the children 'were being well fed on board', 'only had to do light work' and 'did not have to work after sunset'. They wanted the minimum age to go down to at least twelve. Moreover, the boys would not become good fishermen if they were not 'educated' at an early age. Twelve-year-old orphans would come to no good, otherwise, they argued. Plus, the government would have to build a lot more schools, which would cost even more money!

COMPULSORY EDUCATION

Slowly but surely, factory managers and, ultimately, ship owners realized that it was more convenient to employ children who were able to read and write, and who were a little older. Better machines meant that children's small hands were no longer needed. Children were still allowed to work on farms. In 1900, the Lower House passed the Compulsory Education Act, which required children aged between six and twelve

28 CLASS 3 OF A STATE PRIMARY SCHOOL, CA. 1912. KATWIJKS MUSEUM

Kailash Satyarthi, a human rights activist from India who has been fighting child labour since 1980, founded the South Asian Coalition on Child Servitude (SACCS) in 1992. SACCS introduced a 'rug mark' for child-labour-free products and also freed children from workhouses and factories. Despite fierce protests in India, tens of thousands of children were freed.

to be educated, either at school or at home. Only then were the child protection laws finally being enforced. In practice, most parents already sent most of their children to school. There were, of course, exceptions: if girls were needed at home in the household, they were exempted from compulsory education.

But if it was financially necessary, children were taken out of school prematurely, law or no law.

The rise of socialism in the nineteenth century was of course related to the harsh conditions in which people had to survive and to the exploitation of the many by the few.

THE SITUATION TODAY

In the Netherlands, around 10,000 children aged twelve work at least twelve hours a week. Some 9,000 thirteen- and fourteen-year-olds work at least twenty hours a week. They often deliver newspapers, stack shelves in the supermarket, pick bulbs or babysit, but some also do heavy work in factories and on farms. They earn significantly less than the minimum wage: 2.57 euros per hour is the legal wage, and they are often sacked as soon as they become 'too expensive'. The fight for one general minimum wage for everyone, irrespective of age, still goes on.

DEVELOPING COUNTRIES

The situation in developing countries is harrowing. Child labour is widespread in Africa, Asia and South America, not only in agriculture and family businesses, but also in factories and

weaving mills. Poverty is usually the cause of child labour, as was the case in the Netherlands in the nineteenth century, and families are often forced to have their children work or even sell them in order to be able to provide for the primary necessities of life. The difference between child labour and child slavery is not always clear. There are still large companies that do business with companies in these countries that employ children. Increasingly, companies require their suppliers to certify that they have eliminated child labour from their production processes.

In conflict zones, children are used as child soldiers in bloody wars, and are also forced into slavery and prostitution. This must, of course, be brought to an end quickly and relief organisations do what they can, but are often powerless against prejudice and violence.

30 CLASS 4 OF THE STATE PRIMARY SCHOOL, CA. 1910. KATWIJKS MUSEUM

3 CHILDREN IN THE
FISHING INDUSTRY
UP TO 1900

Many children worked on fishing boats at sea and on rivers and inland waterways, as well as in the fishing industry. On board the herring luggers and sloops, the boys (no women or girls, as, according to the seaman's creed, 'a woman and a cliff are a disaster for the ship') had to work even longer hours than the children in the factories, sometimes as long as fifteen to sixteen hours a day. But for the family back home, there was one mouth less to feed. Fishing and hunting had always been male-dominated occupations, which women did not really participate in. Urk was the exception: here, women and girls helped to bring in the seine nets (also called *de zegen*, 'the blessing', because of the prosperity the catch could bring them, see box). Women and girls (and sometimes boys) who worked in the fishing industry usually did other jobs: pickling herring (see box, page 22), rolling herring around gherkins to make *rolmopsen*, peeling shrimp, scrubbing, cooking and pickling mussels, working in oyster sheds and ponds (see box, page 31), cutting the heads off the anchovy and removing the intestines, knitting and repairing nets, walking to markets further away with heavy fish baskets and working in smokehouses (fig. 32) and rope yards. In addition, the women and the older children took care of the (large) family.

Seine nets
Seine fishing is a method where the fish is caught using a net dragged along the sea bed, while performing a gathering manoeuvre.

The *vleet*

A vleet was a long series of drift nets, sometimes 3–4 kilometres (1¾–2½ miles) long, used for herring fishing. The vleet was kept afloat by barrels, the breels, a practice learned from Scottish fishermen in which about fifty air-filled canvas floats called 'Scottish bladders', or blazen, were blown up by the youngest hands on board. A lot of pitch was needed to make them waterproof, as a result of which the boys often had black mouths. The nets were weighted down with weights at the bottom, so that they stood up like a curtain in the sea. The nets were attached to a thick hemp rope, the reep, with thinner ropes. The nets could be raised or lowered, depending on where the herring were.

Working in the fish factories

Women and girls worked in the fish factories and smokehouses (hangens) in towns where lots of Zuiderzee herring was brought in. They filled glass jars with herring by hand, which was then pickled: the good, blue side of the herring had to remain visible, and the fish were neatly stacked on top of each other. They used herring that had already spawned and could no longer be sold as new herring. Rolmopsen (pickled herring wrapped around a gherkin) were rolled by hand. Zuiderzee herring was strung onto smoking sticks by women, girls and boys immediately upon arrival, even if it was at night, to be smoked in hangens. Smoked herring was called bokking and pickled pan-fried herring was called panharing. Everyone ate herring – it was a cheap staple food – and smelled like herring; the smell was very noticeable at church, because when you sweated, it smelled of fish.

32 PUTTING ZUIDERZEE HERRING ON SMOKING STICKS IN A *HANGEN* IN HARDERWIJK. ZUIDERZEE CRAFT FOUNDATION, ENKHUIZEN

FROM FATHER TO SON, FROM MOTHER TO DAUGHTER

It was very common for fishermen to take their sons out fishing at an early age. In fishing villages along the rivers where fishermen would go out on *waalschokkers* and salmon barges, the boys would first come along when they were seven or eight years old. Everyone stayed relatively close to home and would come home after a fishing trip, or at most stay overnight on the boat, or sometimes live on the boat with the whole family. They would be prepared for their future job through play: for example, in Woudrichem children would put a flat stone in the shape of a salmon in a small piece of net. They would then beat the stone, to 'kill' the fish, in the same way the fishermen beat the salmon behind the gills so that it would turn pink. In Kerkdriel, boys played with fish cut out of wood.

We can see the children were put to work very young: the boys in Westervoort had to cut the remains of cut-off willow twigs to braid them into bait baskets. Bait struck onto the hooks of the float lines (see box, page 24), called *prik*, was mainly used by fishermen living along the major rivers and who used longliners (see box, page 24) to fish for haddock and cod on the North Sea and beyond. Elsewhere, things like cooked shrimps or worms were used as bait. In the spring, the children collected oak bark to tan the cotton nets with, in order to make them more sturdy and durable. When the boys went along on proper fishing trips, they learned to hook the bait onto the hooks of the float

Gutting herring

Gutting herring on land has been the custom since the twelfth century, as shown in archaeological finds in the Roskilde Fjord in Denmark. After the invention of gutting herring at sea, around 1400, by Willem Beukelszoon from Biervliet, fishermen could keep herring for longer. Using a sharp gutting knife, the gills, heart, stomach and gallbladder were removed, leaving the pancreatic tissue in the fish (with enzymes to mature the fish meat), which was then cured in brine. Since the invention in Hoorn of the knitted (filet-knotted) herring net in 1416, large numbers of Dutch fishermen started fishing for herring, with so-called haringbuizen and hookers. As a result of the curing process, herring became the nation's favourite food, until right up to the Second World War. Herring was cheap, nutritious, full of protein and could be kept 'fresh' for a reasonable amount of time.

lines – after having bitten off the head of the live *prik* (see fig. 51, page 38) – and lay these out in the rope box, wind the float line onto spools, and keep the board that would be put out for cleaning the nets, the *bungelplank*, steady. They learned to knit and mend nets and bit by bit were taught all the tricks of the trade by their fathers, who had also learned from their fathers. The profession was passed on from father to son, just as the girls learned everything, including knitting, from their mothers (fig. 33).

SOCIAL RELATIONS

Most fishing families from the fishing villages along the Zuiderzee and in Zeeland had their own boat, which was often bought on loan; most of their income would go towards repayment of this debt. These boats could be either flat- or round-bottomed boats, called *botters*, *vletten*, *bonzen*, *aken*, *jollen*, *tjalken*, *blazers*, *hengsten*, *snikken*, *hoogaarzen* etc., and the income depended on what they caught – Zuiderzee herring, flounder, anchovy, smelt, eel, shrimp, plaice, ray, crab, mussels or oysters – how much they caught and what the going rate was, which all varied from year to year and from season to season. Even in winter, they would attempt to catch some fish in the Zuiderzee by cutting a hole in the ice and using dangerous tapping techniques. The investment in and maintenance of the boat and nets and additional expenses, such as the wages of the knocker-up

who would come to your house to wake you up in the middle of the night for a couple of pennies, comprised such a high part of the proceeds that the families rarely managed to lift themselves out of poverty. For their income, the Zuiderzee fishermen

Gutting ban

Until 1704, when their fleet was burnt down by French pirates in the Bay of Lerwick on the Shetland Isles (a loss from which they never recovered), Vlaardingen, Maassluis and Enkhuizen had the exclusive right to gut herring on board their fishing vessels, because this was where the large ports were located in the seventeenth century. The towns got extremely rich from the export of herring to Germany and France. The other fishing villages were banned from gutting herring on board – the landing of gutted herring was strictly forbidden – and were condemned to fishing for fresh fish close to the shore, such as flatfish and roundfish, shrimps and mussels, which had a limited shelf life and had to be sold and consumed immediately.

were completely dependent on the purchase of their Zuiderzee herring by the *hangbazen*, who smoked the herring in sheds called *hangens* and who determined the price (to their advantage, of course). Boys would therefore join the fleet at a young age, and earned barely more than 1 guilder a week.

Boys did heavy work on all ships. For example, Jan Goos from Enkhuizen (see box, page 26) wrote that in 1887, as a nine-year-old, he had to wind the trawling line around the winch with his small hands, in high winds. The line was too thick for his hands and was also covered with poisonous jellyfish tentacles that stung his fingers. He found it very hard. But there was no compassion for children at sea, neither on the barge nor on the lugger: 'Children were valued even less than rotten cabbage at a greengrocer's.' He had to work hard and fast. And after the hard work on board the ship, he also had to bait until eleven o'clock at night. When the weather was fair, he would be busy from four o'clock in the morning until eleven o'clock at night. He would look forward to Saturday, when he could turn in early, because at the end of the week, he could barely keep his eyes open.

34 *BOMSCHUITEN* AT SEA IN *ARRIVAL OF THE FISH* (*AANKOMST VAN DE VIS*). HENDRIK WILLEM MESDAG, 1875. VLAARDINGEN MUSEUM

North Sea Fishing

The situation in the North Sea herring fishing industry, the most important form of fishing around 1900, was very different. Ship owners owned fleets of *bomschuiten* (flat-bottomed vessels that sailed from and landed on the beach, and that were mostly used for fishing close to the shore, fig. 34), sailing luggers (fig. 35) and longliners (fig. 36). These owners were very 'thrifty'. They would try and save money wherever they could, including on the purchase and maintenance of the ships. In order to have more room for the catch, the crew quarters were as small as possible and, at a time without social legislation, the crew's wages would be just as meagre. Fishermen would sign on on these vessels as employees, who did not receive a salary but a percentage of the proceeds of the

fictional story, the situation was very recognizable for the fishing world, because it was quite a realistic representation of reality. The play fuelled the workers' movement, but it took a long time for the situation to change. Several fishing strikes, in 1910 and in the 1930s, also had hardly any impact on the living conditions of fishermen (fig. 37, page 26). It was only after the Second World War that working conditions and pay improved.

catch, which depended on their experience and rank, the so-called *besomming* (see *besomming* on page 39). If the catch was good, then they got to eat; if they caught little or no fish, they would also earn little or nothing. The situation was completely skewed, as the shipowners would always receive the highest return on their investment in the ships and, moreover, only provided part of the victuals (food and drink) on board; the rest, the crew had to bring themselves. The fishermen were away from home for a long time. Each season, running from the beginning of June to the end of November, they would only come home four or five times for a few days. On board, they would work fourteen to sixteen hours a day and once in the port they could not go home straight away. First, the fish had to be unloaded and the nets had to be stored away, work for which they would not get paid extra.

Shipowners sometimes kept the ships in such a bad state of repair that they would go down with all men on board; the owners would claim the insurance money, leaving the widows and dependants in poverty at a time when they were dependent on charity because there were no widows' and orphans' pensions. However, some funds were set up that would provide widows with a small sum of money.

In 1900, Herman Heijermans based his play *The Good Hope* (*Op hoop van zegen*) on these skewed relationships. In it, Kniertje, whose husband and two sons have already 'stayed' at sea, loses her two remaining younger sons after their badly maintained ship perishes and, in order to survive, is forced to work as a maid for the ship owner who had caused all her misery. Although it was a

36 LONGLINER MD 10 FROM MIDDELHARNIS. ORIGIN UNKNOWN

POVERTY

Poor fishing families usually lived in tiny, dank houses, often with no more than one or two rooms – the second of which was usually a small alcove – a hallway, a kitchenette and a loft. They not only lived there, but also worked and stored their fishing gear there. Up to five or six children would sleep in a box bed, while the parents slept in the alcove. Infants sometimes slept in a drawer under their parents' beds. People were prudish, and children were kept separate if one of the others had to wash themselves (which only happened on Saturdays). There was no birth control, most fishermen and workers were not formally educated and they had little knowledge other than what they learnt

37 FISHERY STRIKE IN THE 1930S. KATWIJKS MUSEUM

and everyone had to peel until the evening. The
shells and fish waste were fed to the pig(s), which
almost every fisherman's wife kept as a type of
'piggy bank' for bad times. A few weeks before the
pigs were slaughtered – if there was any money –
the shrimp shells and fish waste were replaced by
flour, to prevent the meat from tasting like fish.
Young children learned to knit and mend nets at
a very early age. They first had to fill the needles
with cotton yarn and then knit nets in the evening
after dinner.

in practice. Therefore, families were large.
Mortality for infants and small children, who
often had to be cared for by the slightly older
children because their mothers also worked,
was high.

Everyone, tiny or tall, young or old, had to work
to supplement the family income. In many houses
the front room was converted into a small shop,
where the mother or grandmother tried to earn
some money. But because there were many of these
shops they would not earn that much. Peeling
shrimp was another way to earn an extra income,
and the entire family would pitch in. After school,
the cooked shrimps would be piled up on the table

38 FISHERMEN'S HOUSES IN SCHEVENINGEN, CA. 1920. HAAGS GEMEENTEARCHIEF

39 FISHERMEN ON THE ZUIDERHAVENDIJK IN ENKHUIZEN, CA. 1920.
ZUIDERZEE CRAFT FOUNDATION, ENKHUIZEN

40 BALLING UP SKEINED WOOL IN VOLENDAM. LAU SOMBROEK,
VOLENDAM

The whole family sometimes earned some extra money by picking peas. Picking a sack of peas (approximately 100 litres) would earn them 60 cents. Small children, mainly girls, would also pick apart old rope, so that the fibres could be used to fill up cracks in the ships. It would take a week to fill up a large bag, which paid 50 cents. In Katwijk, fishing families would hull beans for the canning factory, or glue stickers onto pillboxes for the doctor and the pharmacist at night. People felt guilty when they were sitting still or doing nothing; their hands always had to do something!

In addition to all the other chores, they also made their own clothes. Girls and women would knit vests, stockings, mittens and sweaters (fig. 40, 41, 42). Mothers would place a pin in the knitting where the girls worked to, so they could determine how many rows they had knitted that day. Girls regularly moved the pin down a few rows so it looked as if they had knitted more, hoping to fool their mothers. But the mothers were not born yesterday, of course.

Hidden treats

Some mothers made the hard and seemingly endless work children had to do a little more attractive by putting a few pennies in between the shrimps, peas or inside a ball of wool as a reward.

41 *THE KNITTER (HET BREISTERTJE)*, AFTER AN ENGRAVING BY J.H. RENNEFELD
FROM *DE KINDEREN DER ZEE*, POEMS BY NICOLAAS BEETS, AROUND 1900.

43 THE KATWIJK FISHING SCHOOL, FOUNDED BY MASTER BOORSMA, CA. 1920

FOOD AND DRINK

Food was simple and consisted mainly of carbohydrates and proteins. They ate the fish, mussels or shrimp they caught themselves, rye bread (wheat was too expensive due to excise duty), gruel and lots of boiled potatoes, sometimes with a gravy of melted butter and vinegar or mustard and vinegar. The fish could be anything, often undersized fish that could not be sold and was therefore eaten at home. Meat was rarely or never eaten and vegetables, except cabbage, were not on the menu either. The smaller children got the smallest portion and the older you got, the bigger your piece of bread was. Stealing or secretly swapping food with siblings was usually severely punished: they would be sent to bed without food. Sweets were a rarity – on Sundays, they would get half a spiced cookie and a boiled sweet on birthdays. People did not have a refrigerator, so in order to keep food longer it was fermented by salting it (such as sauerkraut) or pickling it in vinegar. If vegetables were on the menu, they would sometimes be cooked for three hours or even longer. In order to add a bit of taste, they were generously sprinkled with salt. The cupboards were mostly empty. Drinking water was taken from wells, and was not always clean. In the countryside, houses were not connected to the water mains. Poor drinking water caused diseases such as cholera, and resulted in quite a few deaths. The alternative was tea, coffee (or something that was called coffee) and alcoholic beverages such as beer and gin. The second cup of coffee or tea was always drunk without sugar. Alcoholism, and the cost of drinking, led to a great deal of misery and unrest.

42 KNITTING GIRLS FROM VOLENDAM. LAU SOMBROEK, VOLENDAM

28

EDUCATION

At the end of the nineteenth century, people started to realize that it was important to offer young fishermen, from the age of sixteen, more training, so that they would have a better insight into the theoretical side of fishing. For the older children, who had several years of practical experience, such training was interesting. After a few years of working as a sailor and with a diploma, they could achieve the rank of mate or even ultimately that of skipper. In 1878, the first fishing school was established in Scheveningen.

Navigation was an important part of the training, because collisions and the inability to locate telegraph cables underwater resulted in a lot of damage. Learning to sail and work with sailing and fishing gear, making knots and splicing cables were, of course, the most important elements of the training, because only sailing vessels were used. Initially, the education system was mainly nautically oriented. Little attention was paid to knowledge of fish and fishing equipment. When the steam lugger was introduced, engine knowledge also became important. In 1902, the Katwijk fishing school was founded with the help of the well-known local teacher, Kornelis Boorsma (1825-1915) (fig. 43). In addition to being the founder, Master Boorsma also became the first school principal, although he was already in his eighties. The fishing school offered evening classes for boys between the ages of fourteen and seventeen, who attended school during the four winter months from January to April. They worked during the day and in the evening took lessons in navigation, splicing and mending nets. From May until the end of the herring season, they would work on the herring luggers.

The girls who knitted or mended the nets were also trained, for example at the fishing school in Vlaardingen (fig. 44).

44 LEARNING TO MEND NETS AT THE FISHING SCHOOL IN THE TRADE BUILDING ON THE PARALLELWEG IN VLAARDINGEN, CA. 1920

4 AT SEA

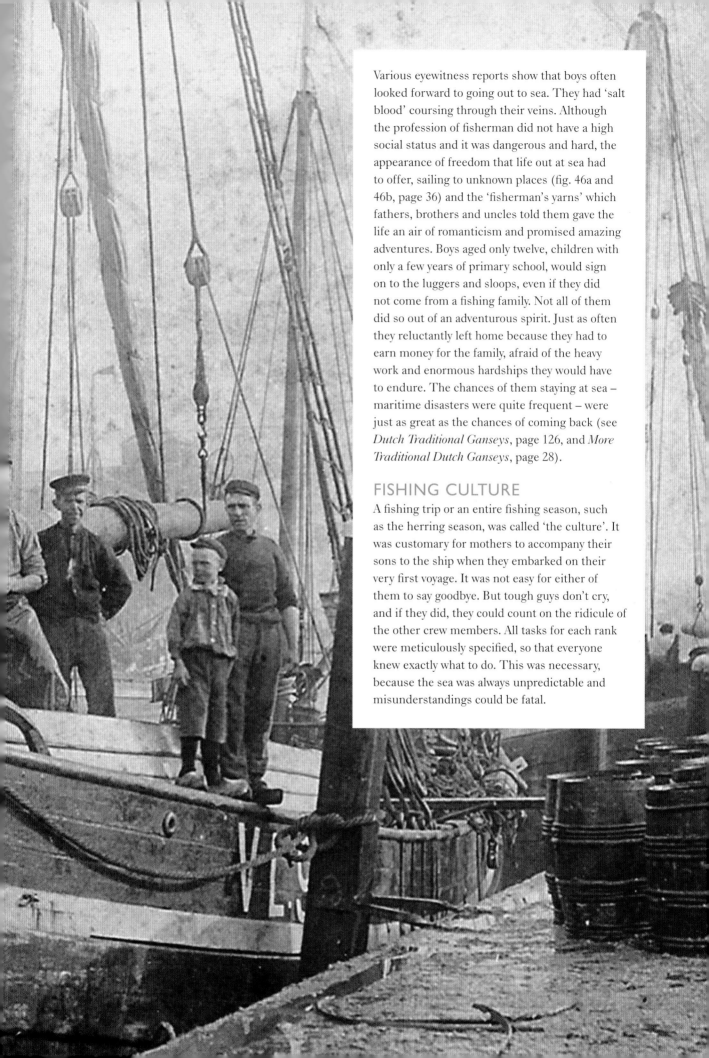

Various eyewitness reports show that boys often looked forward to going out to sea. They had 'salt blood' coursing through their veins. Although the profession of fisherman did not have a high social status and it was dangerous and hard, the appearance of freedom that life out at sea had to offer, sailing to unknown places (fig. 46a and 46b, page 36) and the 'fisherman's yarns' which fathers, brothers and uncles told them gave the life an air of romanticism and promised amazing adventures. Boys aged only twelve, children with only a few years of primary school, would sign on to the luggers and sloops, even if they did not come from a fishing family. Not all of them did so out of an adventurous spirit. Just as often they reluctantly left home because they had to earn money for the family, afraid of the heavy work and enormous hardships they would have to endure. The chances of them staying at sea – maritime disasters were quite frequent – were just as great as the chances of coming back (see *Dutch Traditional Ganseys*, page 126, and *More Traditional Dutch Ganseys*, page 28).

FISHING CULTURE

A fishing trip or an entire fishing season, such as the herring season, was called 'the culture'. It was customary for mothers to accompany their sons to the ship when they embarked on their very first voyage. It was not easy for either of them to say goodbye. But tough guys don't cry, and if they did, they could count on the ridicule of the other crew members. All tasks for each rank were meticulously specified, so that everyone knew exactly what to do. This was necessary, because the sea was always unpredictable and misunderstandings could be fatal.

ON THE LUGGERS

The crew of a herring lugger consisted of thirteen, fourteen or fifteen men: from high to low these were the captain, the mate, the engine operator or mechanic (on a steam lugger), five sailor-fishermen, the sailor-cook, the young sailor, referred to as the '7/8th', the eldest (one or two), the youngest, the rigger (*reepschieter*) and the spacer (*afhouder*), of which four or five were boys between the ages of twelve and fifteen who had to work as hard as the older sailors.

Spacer

You started out as a twelve-year-old on a lugger as a spacer, or *afhouder* (see box, page 33), who, as the greenhorn, was assigned heavy duties. With his still immature body he had to guide thick ropes, shovel coal for the cook, take care of drinking water and do cleaning work. He was the older crew members' play thing, and not only did they exercise their authority, but they were also not averse to bullying. On many occasions, this resulted in the youngest crew members hiding or fleeing the ship after arriving on the Shetland Islands, where the herring migration would start, never to come back (see the box on page 117 in *Dutch Traditional Ganseys* and the box on page 23 in *More Traditional Dutch Ganseys*). If they had survived everything on a first journey – sea sickness (using an empty clog to be sick in), sleeping in the tip of the ship, called 'hell', where the swell was greatest, being plagued by rats and fleas, having to do heavy work including chopping ice and shovelling coal, little sleep, dangerous and cold weather, rough seas, homesickness and bullying – they were considered a man and rewarded with a box of cigars when they returned home. In many pictures, you see boys posing with a box of cigars. At the time it was thought that smoking was healthy and kept pests at bay (fig. 47, page 37).

Rigger

If you had endured your first year on a herring lugger, you would be promoted to rigger, or *reepschieter*. A rigger was usually a small, lean boy going out to sea for the second year (but sometimes still on his first sign-up) – or, as was also said, for a second culture (fishing season). He was the one-but-lowest in rank. He had to carefully stow away the rigging, the *reep*, to which the nets were attached, sitting in a dedicated spot in the stern, the *reepkee*. It was important that the *reep* did not get caught when the 2–3 kilometre (1¼–1¾ mile) long nets were put out again. To invoke the higher powers as the nets were put out the crew would call out '*op hoop van zegen*' ('in good hope').

Youngest

The next person up was the youngest. A youngest, together with the sailor-cook, would guide the nets in below deck into the bilges, one on the port side and one on the starboard side. Half the *vleet* (the herring nets) would be stored in either room. When coiling the nets, the youngest was responsible for the floats (*blazen*), which he, the spacer and the rigger had blown up. Because of the tar used to make the floats watertight, the boys' faces were black as soot after blowing them up. When the herring was being gutted, he had to bring the filled basket (which had three handles) to where the herring was mixed with salt in a *warrebak* (a wooden container). The youngest would stay above-deck on the look-out at mealtimes. After meals, he would clean the kettles and boilers. He would make coffee and bring it to the below-deck room at the stern where the captain, mate and engine operator were. Together with the rigger and spacer, he would clean the crew quarters, with the youngest being responsible for fetching the *puzze*, a bucket on a rope filled with sea water. The spacer and rigger would do most of the cleaning.

Because the nets were often hauled in at night and the sailors would go back to their bunks during the day, the spacer, rigger and youngest had to stay up. To ensure they did not make too much noise, they were not allowed in the front, and had to stay above-deck, whatever the weather. They also had other tasks, such as frying fish, shovelling coal for the cook, hacking ice and cleaning the crew quarters, the *voorin*. The quarters were where the crew would sleep – apart from the captain, mate and, in later years, the engine operator, who had their own rooms at the stern – and where meals were prepared.

The youngest would not be on sentry duty; that was too much of a responsibility for them. Not only were the lugger and crew at stake, but the *vleet* could get caught up, crossed over by other boats or get tangled with other *vleets*.

This story about life on board a Vlaardingen lugger was written in 1957 by Frans Stam (1885–1965). He started on this ship in 1897 at the age of twelve, as a spacer (afhouder), the youngest crew member. His granddaughter Francisca Stam sent it to the Vlaardingen Museum.

'My first ship was a lugger from Pot, the Slikkeveer 11, VL 40. It was one of the smallest luggers of that time. We could take on twenty-two loads: twenty-two times seventeen barrels of herring. It was one of the last luggers with a douwspil (hand-driven axle). The rigging had to be taken in pulling on spokes and wrapped around a capstan. The fifteen crew were: the captain, the mate, the cook, seven sailors and five boys, namely two eldest, one youngest, one rigger and one spacer. The captain and the mate had a separate cabin on the stern, the other thirteen lived in the fore. That was a square space, tapered towards the front, following the body of the ship. Along the walls were benches, with the stop boxes underneath (see *Stop Box and Clothing, page 39*), which contained the provisions the shipping company did not provide, such as butter, sugar, condensed milk, cheese etc. There was no table, but there was a large stove in the middle of the room, the galley. On the walls hung oilskins and the other items of clothing of the crew; wardrobes had not yet been invented, and there would not have been room for one either. Underwear, wrapped up in a pillowcase, was stored under your pillow, dirty underwear was put in another pillowcase and also stored under the pillow, or at the foot of the bed. There was no time or room to wash clothes, by the way, and drinking water, which was taken on when mooring in a port in the usual new herring barrels, had to be used sparingly.'

Drinking water

'About that drinking water; it could take on all kinds of colours and smells. If the barrels were sealed properly, and little or no light could enter, it would soon begin to smell and turn blue.

'If they were not sealed, the water would leak out and sometimes they would empty completely after a while. Sometimes the new barrels had staves on the inside that were still somewhat black, because they had been held over a fire to bend them, resulting in black water. After putting a hot poker in water, the colour would disappear.'

Sleeping berths

'There were only three one-man cages in the frondel (fore) and five two-man cages. Of course the five boys had to share one cage. This was far from ideal, especially when someone was seasick, which was common. I myself shared the bed with an old man, about fifty years old, which was quite odd at that time. I was spared seasickness, given the circumstances, but then came the fleas. I couldn't lie still, and I almost daren't move, because my cage mate would then scold me for waking him up: "lie still you, you're kicking me." The old man seemed to be immune to the little pests.'

45 IN THE CAGE ON A HERRING LUGGER. KATWIJKS MUSEUM

Coal hell

'The cook was my boss and my work consisted of sweeping the floor, emptying spit bins, shovelling coal for the galley, etc. I had to dig the coals from a box under the floor of the forecastle, called coal hell. It really was hell on earth. Most of the coal was fine, and I needed the coarser pieces to light the stove, which I had to pick out with a shovel and scoop.'

Brown beans, pea soup, peas and grits

'In the afternoon, the three youngest boys, the youngest, the rigger and the spacer, had to eat up on deck. There was not enough space downstairs, because the captain and the mate, who stayed in the aft, also ate in the forecastle in the afternoon and evening. We would try and find a sheltered place on the aft deck. As the youngest, I then had to haul the food up to the deck through the hole in the frondel in a wooden box. The menu consisted of brown beans twice a week, pea soup twice a week, grey peas once a week, grits with syrup once a week and potatoes (as long as stocks lasted) with fried herring on Saturday. Otherwise, we had rancid bacon. It happened more than once that when the weather was quite bad, sea water had gushed into the box of food before I got to where we were sitting. I would then give the food to the fish, and I had to go back with the empty box to beg for another portion, sometimes getting cursed at as well. One day, the weather was so bad that we decided to eat in the cabin, which happened to be empty, because it was impossible to do on deck. I don't know where we got the courage from, but there was a delicious piece of half-sweet cheese lying on the table, and we all cut off a big chunk and ate it. "What's the worst that can happen to us," the rigger said. When our theft was discovered, the captain immediately wanted to give us a beating, but the mate, a quiet man, stopped him, and we got away with it. The mate (God bless his soul) took us to one side and told us: "In future, you can eat in the cabin in bad weather and I'll take responsibility, but don't touch anything and make sure you don't leave any traces."

'There were no toilets on the luggers, all you had was a barrel (with a rope attached, so that you could rinse it after use) if you had to do a "number two". That's not what we called it then, we called it "throwing out some bait" or "extending your spine with a dotted line", but the most popular term was simply "taking a shit".'

The fishing grounds
'After five days, we arrived at the fishing grounds and cast out the nets, called the vleet, for the first time. The vleet consisted of seventy-five nets, all connected to each other. Each net was about 33 metres (100 feet) long. The width or depth of each net was about 8 metres (26¼ feet). The nets were connected to the reep (a thick rope) at equal distances as the nets were long, using 5.5 metres (18 feet) long seizings. Along the reep, the breels were attached using breeltouwen, again about 5.5 metres (18 feet) in length. The vleet, reep, etc. then slowly sank to the sea floor, until the whole thing hung on the breeld – barrels that tapered towards the top, which would float on the water. At half past midnight, we started to pull in the vleet. The youngest, the rigger and the spacer were woken up half an hour earlier, because they had to be on deck first. The spilloopers then took up their positions on the spokes to wind in the reep. The number of spilloopers varied according to the force of the wind and sea, from three to seven, because while taking in the nets, the ship would be facing the wind. The spacer would sit on a bench under the axle, to "hold off" the reep and guide it to the special hold, where the rigger would store it away. The youngest was in front and would loosen the breels and seizings from the reep. The rest of the crew was on the midship, hauling in the nets. Taking in the vleet, again depending on the weather, took between three and seven hours, during which time we did not get coffee or anything; the vleet had to be in first.

'As soon as the vleet was on board, we had a breakfast with hard sea cookies and weak coffee. Coffee and tea were boiled in a large copper kettle, coffee in the mornings and tea in the afternoons. Dinner invariably consisted of rice and fried herring. The herring caught was gutted, salted in barrels and stowed in the holds.

'It continued like this and we did five journeys that summer, and caught a total of a hundred loads, equalling 1,700 barrels of herring, which was not a bad catch, but the prices were mediocre. This was my first sea voyage as a herring fisherman. The season began early June and ended at the end of November. I came aboard full of enthusiasm and cheer, having read books by Michiel de Ruyter, etc. But in the beginning I shed many a bitter tear, I was simply desperate, with all that cursing and yelling, and as a twelve-year-old boy I was so affected by everything. Every journey I swore was my last, but I still felt proud every time we would sail into port with our catch. Luckily, my skin got thicker and thicker, and in the end nothing touched me anymore. I did my job as well as I could, and for the rest I didn't care about anything, I just kept sailing and became a captain myself at the age of twenty-five.'

Courtesy of Vlaardingen Museum and Francisca Stam, Frans Stam's granddaughter.

A Little Rigger

The Katwijk luggers are ready to go out to sea and start their journey. Around eleven o'clock, the signal for departure is given. Everyone says their goodbyes for a few weeks. The luggers blow their ship's horns loudly. This is how the career of a sailor starts, of a small, hopeful fourteen-year-old boy from Leiden, starting out as a rigger, under the supervision of the cook, having no idea what to expect. Not much later, passing the piers of IJmuiden, the lugger puts its head into the wind and immediately starts to swing and pound, because there is a considerable swell, and the foam sweeps over the deck with the ever rising waves. The rigger, who doesn't have sea legs yet, starts to feel unwell. The cook calls him inside. 'Come on glibber, get to work, you can get seasick in your own time.' When he's finished his work, he can go down to the forecastle, where he immediately climbs into his cage to go to sleep, as he feels horrible. He had expected it to be totally different. But on board a herring lugger, schadenfreude is the best form of entertainment there is.

The young rigger has to do nasty jobs for the sailors, and in the meantime he is being taunted with the remark: 'We called out De Hoop (the hospital ship) for you and it will take you back to shore.' He is lucky, they have to sail two days before they arrive at the fishing grounds. He has some time to recover from his seasickness. When it's time for dinner, he is pulled out of his cage; food is good for him, the sailors say with a grin on their faces.

The first evening is a breeze for the crew, they only have to guard the helm. The rest can go to sleep. They work six-hour shifts. The crew can now have a 'farmer's night' and sleep for six hours. For the rigger this is a great comfort, because the youngest crew members are exempt from the helm guard at night.

On the third day after their departure from IJmuiden, they arrive at their fishing grounds near Scotland around noon. The ship slows down until it comes to a standstill. The captain says he wants to put out the nets around four o'clock. The rigger and spacer have to keep guard and make sure that tea is ready at half past three. Then they have to wake up the crew, who are still asleep (not a pleasant job), so they can shoot the vleet in time (throw it overboard).

The nets are pulled up out of the net hold by two sailors. The white floats, with one blue float for every eighth net, are attached to the nets. The mate ties the seizing (the rope that connects the nets to the reep) to the reep that comes out of the hold and everything is put overboard. The captain takes off his cap when the first net hits the sea, bends over the bulwark and shouts: 'Gestrekt, vooruit maaaar…op hoop van Zegen!' (Straight on you gooooo…In good hope!) The shooting of the vleet takes about three quarters of an hour. The spacer calls out after the freshly shot vleet: 'Geschoten met vlijt, God zegen onze arbeid.' (Shot with diligence, God bless our work.) Once the vleet is in the sea, everyone has time to eat and take a nap, except for the watchman. Once the vleet is shot, the rigger has to fry fish, herring and mackerel, which takes some time. Whatever the weather, even during a heavy storm, this has to be done!

At one in the morning, the vleet is hauled in again. The watchman wakes the crew from their deep sleep. They eat something and drink coffee. Then they go on deck. The rigger is lowered into the rope hold, and the spacer sits down behind the donkey (winches/hoists that pull the reep in). At the head of the ship, the nets are pulled off the reep, while two speer-reephaalders pull the nets on board. The five wantstanders ('sailors') pull the nets in a bit more and shake the herring out of the nets. The cook and his mate in the hold pull the nets over the roll and these are neatly laid down.

The rigger stores the reep in elliptical loops, while the spacer behind the winches guides the reep into the hold. The captain makes sure that the lugger moves slowly forward, so that the nets are pushed out and up by the sea, as it were. If there are little herring in nets, it takes about three hours to haul in the vleet of sixty nets. Halfway through hauling in the vleet it is time for a 'cuppa' and a bite to eat. With large catches, for example eighty to ninety barrels, the crew has to work for about twelve hours at a time. When the vleet is on board, the catch must be gutted and processed.

COMMERCIAL STREET, LERWICK

R. H. Ramsey Photographer. Lerwick

46A COMMERCIAL STREET, LERWICK, SHETLAND ISLANDS. SHETLAND MUSEUM & ARCHIVES

Eldest

Above the youngest was the eldest, of whom there were usually two. The eldest had four to five years of experience and were given greater responsibilities. While one eldest would help get the *vleet* out at night, the other eldest would be at the helm. They would change roles during the shift. Before taking in the *vleet* early in the morning, the two eldest would set up the *last* on deck: a system of long planks in between the cribs (*krebbes*) on the port and starboard sides, where the herring would be emptied into from the nets. When taking in the nets, the eldest would put the back sail – the so-called *gatzeil* – in the correct position and helped the sailors to gut the herring. They also helped fill up and store the barrels filled with herring in the hold. One of the eldest would traditionally bake pancakes on Saturday evening.

ON THE LONGLINERS

A longliner would have smaller crew than a lugger, normally a crew of twelve. The longline, which had cross-lines with hooks on them, the *repen* or *sneuen*, was mainly used to catch fresh fish such as haddock and cod. These were stored alive in a bun with hopper plates, with holes to let water flow through it.

46B DUTCH FISHERMEN IN COMMERCIAL STREET, LERWICK, SHETLAND ISLANDS. SHETLAND MUSEUM & ARCHIVES

Koffiekoker/speeljongen or prikkenbijter

On a sloop, the youngest crew member was called a *koffiekoker/speeljongen* or *prikkenbijter* (fig. 48, 49). On a sloop from Middelharnis, the youngest was called *koffiekoker* (coffee maker), because one of his tasks was to take care of coffee and tea. The origin of the name *speeljongen* (playboy) is not entirely clear, but it – rather controversially – suggests that the boy was a 'plaything', bullied by the older crew members on board. The 'sea father', one of the older crew members, would keep an eye on him and take him under his wing. For bait on the hooks, they often used *prik*, or lamprey, eel-like, jawless fish, which were kept alive in trays (fig. 50). If baiting had to be done, the *speeljongen* – also called *prikkenbijter* (bait biter) – would, under the supervision of the captain, use his canines to bite the lamprey's head to kill it (fig. 51). This was

49 BELOW: *KOFFEKOKER* KEES VAN DER SLUIS FROM MIDDELHARNIS. GOEREE-OVERFLAKKEE REGIONAL ARCHIVE

47 SPACER FROM EGMOND WITH A CIGAR. VLAARDINGEN CITY ARCHIVES

48 STATUE OF A *KOFJEKOKER* (COFFEE MAKER) IN THE PORT OF IJMUIDEN

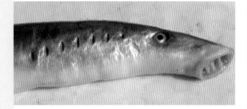

necessary so that the captain could cut the lifeless fish into smaller pieces. This was such dirty work that every so few hundred bites the *prikkenbijter* would get some figs or something else to eat to get rid of the foul taste.

51 *PRIKKENBIJTER* AND A FISHERMAN, CA. 1910. VLAARDINGEN MUSEUM

Inbakker and omtoor

After two years, you would become an *inbakker* (fig. 52). When fishing on longliners, he would ensure that the lines of the longliner would not get tangled up when taking them in and storing them in the boxes (*inbakken*), so that the nets could be deployed again quickly (comparable to the rigger). At fourteen or fifteen, he was given the rank of *omtoor*. He would already have been working on a longliner for about two years. His job was to help guide the *jonen*, a type of bobber-buoy-beacon in one, to keep the longlines, which could be up to 12 kilometres (7½ miles) long, still. During the catch, the *omtoor* had to decapitate the cod that was caught and remove the gills. That is why he was also called *onthoofder*, or 'decapitator'. Furthermore, the *omtoor*, together with the *inbakker* and the *speeljongen*, helped to keep the deck and holds clean.

MENTAL AND PHYSICAL WELL-BEING

Religion played an important role in the lives of fishermen, partly because of the uncertainty of the profession. In order to educate the youngest crew members on board, they received confirmation classes from the eldest or the captain. During the culture, fishermen would attend the Dutch church in Lerwick on the Shetland Islands on Sundays, or when they were out at sea, go to the hospital vessel *De Hoop*, which always sailed close to the fleets, just like the naval vessels that kept an eye on the ships. Sick or injured fishermen were reported to *De Hoop* via flag signals (fishing vessels did not have radio yet), taken off board, nursed and returned when possible so that they could continue their work.

FOOD

Food, or victuals, was partly provided by the shipping company. The ship would have rations on board, such as potatoes, vegetables, condensed milk, oatmeal, rice and *zeekaak* (a type of hard sea biscuit), provided by the shipping company, but the fishermen had to buy certain other items, such as cheese, sugar and butter, themselves (fig. 53). The mainstay of their food was, of course, fish, which was available in large quantities, and very healthy because of the natural fats. The fish was usually pan-fried and eaten as a group from the pan, which is why it was also called *pannenvis* – 'pan fish'. In addition, the diet consisted of pulses, such as brown beans, field peas and green peas or a bean and pea soup with rice or grits, potato and

52 *INBAKKER* ON BOARD A LONGLINER. VLAARDINGEN MUSEUM

SOORT DER GOEDEREN.	TAKS	1ste REIS.	2de REIS.	3de REIS.	4de REIS.	5de REIS.
SLA-OLIE		1.				
ELIXER			½	½		
JOPENBIER		1.				
		50		50		
MOSTERD		4.		2		
PETROLEUM		80.		80		
KAARSEN	pak	2.				
SPECERIJEN						
AARDAPPELS		7		5		
MOPPEN ENZ.		3.				
BEZEMS		2+6				
ROZIJNEN	kg			11		
MELK		2+4.		4		
BESSENSAP						
TERPETIJN		2.				
ZEEP EN SODA		2+2.	2	2		
ROET	kg	4.	2	2		
REUZEL	kg	10.	10	10		
KOLEN	kg	4000				
DWEILEN		3.	2	2		
TURF						
BAKKEN						
LAMPEGLAZEN						
LAMPEKATOEN						
BLAASPIJPEN		12.	6			
MESSEN		12.	6			
		12.	12			

N.V. Zeevisscherij Mij. en Haringhandel
voorheen A. VERBOON.

De bemanning bestaat uit 12 koppen.

53 COMMISSIONS LIST OF HERRING LUGGER *EBEN HAEZER*. STADSARCHIEF VLAARDINGEN

sometimes bacon. Fishermen would eat oatmeal or rice porridge, made with cans of condensed milk. Apart from smoked bacon, other meat was too perishable and therefore not on the menu. Fresh vegetables and fresh milk were used for as long as they could be kept fresh, but after the first week, meals would primarily consist of peas and beans. Besides *zeekaak*, the fisherman ate a bread-cake called *broeder* which was made from a mixture of flour, beer or milk and yeast, currants and raisins, cooked in a bag and eaten warm with some sugar or syrup. Sometimes they would bake bread and there was margarine or butter on board. On Saturday night, one of the eldest would make pancakes. Sailors would drink a lot of coffee, tea and beer. The provisions on the luggers varied, and those from Vlaardingen were much better than on those from Katwijk, for example.

BESOMMING

About 25 per cent of the *besomming* (the proceeds of a fishing trip or the proceeds of a fishing season or culture) were divided among the crew, after deduction of the fixed costs. This percentage is an assumption, because it would differ tremendously in the course of time. It was not until 1923 that the trade unions managed to negotiate a guaranteed wage of 10 guilders a week; until then, fishermen and their families had to wait and see if they would bring home any money or not. It was for good reason that they called the old system 'sailing in good hope', a reference to fate and God's mercy. All crew members were given a fixed part of the *besomming* based on their position, so it was fairly easy to calculate how much someone had earned after each voyage. The amount was converted into eighths via a particular mathematical system. A captain would receive 16/8, or 3.5 per cent of the total besomming, the mate 12/8, the engine operator 10/8, a sailor 8/8, a young sailor 7/8, the eldest 6/8, the youngest 5/8, the rigger 4/8 and the spacer 3/8. Crew members were also referred to by their percentage of the *besomming*.

After the Second World War, fishing became an attractive profession for young boys, partly because the pay was good. Around 1950, a spacer would on average earn 29 guilders (13.20 euros) per week and a rigger 39 guilders. The youngest and eldest would be paid 48 and 58 guilders, respectively. By way of comparison, a young factory worker earned 17 or 18 guilders a week at the time, and the average disposable family income in the Netherlands was 50 guilders a week.

STOP BOX AND CLOTHING

Straw for sleeping was provided by the ship owner and was placed in a blue and white gingham mattress cover, called a *schuddetijk*. A fisherman's personal items, including a gutting knife, repair kit, Bible, smoking equipment, candy, biscuits and cake were stored in a stop box or *stoppenkist*, which was often beautifully decorated with paintwork and carvings (fig. 54). A fisherman had to provide his own clothing. His outfit consisted of various

54 STOP BOX FROM KATWIJK. KATWIJKS MUSEUM

parts. The gansey was usually worn as top layer, but sometimes under a coat of thick woollen cloth or, at sea in rough weather, under oilskin. Fishermen would also have a sou'wester, a kas or tunic, *casjacs* (a kind of smock), long oilskin trousers and sleeves, and corduroy pants with front flap. They also wore *salpatters* or spats around their shoes, sea boots or clogs, to protect them against the grease and dirt. The outfit included an apron or cloth with or without flap, sweaters, shirts, long black jackets, long-sleeved, madder-dyed flannel undershirts (fig. 55) which were supposed to protect them against rheumatism (which a study by the Academic Hospital in Leiden confirmed), English leather trousers, leather sleeves, sleeve straps, belts, stockings, blue trousers, jackets, smocks and tan-coloured boiler suits and trousers. In winter, they wore a flannel shirt and a knit vest of thick wool under the gansey. Thick, double woven long underpants were essential in winter. If you fell over, it was hard to get up again. In summer, a zipper was often inserted in older sweaters that had thinned a bit due to wear.

The fishermen wore large knitted or felted mittens made of wool (fig. 56), to prevent hand injuries when hauling in nets or longlines, which had lots of hooks (see box, page 24). Usually, the mittens had a thumb on either side, so that you could always put one on the right way and the thumbs would not wear as quickly. Fishermen wore headgear – hats, caps, beanies, tams – which varied from place to place.

55 SHIRT DYED WITH MADDER. KATWIJKS MUSEUM

56 FELTED MITTENS WITH TWO THUMBS. MUSEUM SPAKENBURG

A ketelbinkie *worked on commercial vessels, where his position was comparable to that of a spacer on a herring logger and a koffiekoker/inbakker on a longliner. Because the song named after him is so well-known in the Netherlands, and describes the difficult existence of such children at sea in such a touching manner, I want to include it here.*

Ketelbinkie
*When we left the port of Rotterdam,
on the Edam, an old barge,
with cockroaches in the midship
and rat nests in the fore,
we had a little boy on board
that was our Ketelbink
It was his first time out at sea
he had never heard of sharks...
At the quayside back home
he had timidly said goodbye to his mum,
He hadn't dared to kiss her,
this street kid from Rotterdam...*

*He was scolded by the stokers
because from the very first day,
as soon as we left the pier,
he got seasick and retired to the forecastle...
With gin and lemons
they got him back on his legs,
as seasick crew only cost money
and damaged the cargo...
When, carrying his kettles with hot water,
from the galley to the fore,
he looked like a desperate wreck,
this street kid from Rotterdam...*

*When he finally got to go to bed,
and fell asleep after a long day,
the watchman would scold him
for crying for his mother...
One beautiful morning,
somewhere in the Pacific,
while they were shouting for their coffee,
he never got out of his bunk...
And when the mate went to him
carrying quinine and miracle oil,
he asked for an advance on his wages,
for the old lady in Rotterdam...*

*In sail cloth and a heavy grate
they laid him on the hatch.
The captain lifted his cap
and with a groggy voice said the prayer...
And after the 'One, two, three in God's name!'
the Ketelbinkie went overboard,
who didn't dare kiss his old mother,
because that was not what sailors did...
The man had an extra shot that night,
and sent the old mother a telegram.
That was the end of a 'sailor',
this street kid from Rotterdam...*

Many people sing, 'Toen wij <u>*uit*</u> *Rotterdam vertrokken'. The Dutch text, however, reads, 'Toen wij* <u>*van*</u> *Rotterdam vertrokken.' This minor difference indicates the desire to come back to the place, not leave it forever. The song contains quite a few sailor terms that are no longer generally known and used. Foc'sle (pronounced as 'foksel') is the slang version of the English word 'forecastle', the place behind the bow where the crew slept.*

5 KNITTING

SAGATHY

Because of the ban on imports of wool and to keep clothes affordable, ganseys and other garments were mainly knitted using (belly) wool from the domestic sheep from Texel, the Texelaar. This wool was called sagathy, possibly after a peddler with that name or derived from *saai*, a woollen woven fabric made from belly wool. This is opposed to worsted yarn, which was made from the best back wool. The wool was sold door to door by peddlers.

Sagathy cannot be compared to any yarns currently on the market. The Texelaar was not a wool sheep, like the merino sheep, originally from Spain, but a sheep kept for its milk and meat. In the Netherlands, sagathy was predominantly spun in Veenendaal, Leiden and the province of North Brabant. Because of the short fibre, a strongly twisted yarn was first spun in the spinning mill or by home spinners, to obtain sufficient strength. Next, two to five of these threads were twisted at the factory into sagathy with various thicknesses (two-, three-, four- and five-ply). After this, sagathy was dyed and then wrapped onto cards or skeined up. Sagathy had a beautiful sheen because of the lanolin, the natural wool fat, which was not completely washed out and was also added during spinning as spinning oil. This made the yarn warmer and more water repellent, too.

The pure Texelaar sheep from that time no longer exists; the variety has been crossbred with other varieties in order to obtain better characteristics. Colour numbers, as we use them today, did not exist at the time, so each batch of wool was different in colour. People would knit with whatever yarn was available. Depending on the local preference and the price of the yarn, they could choose between dark blue yarn, dyed with indigo or Nassaus blue; Nassaus beige yarn, which also contained red fibre; cornflower-blue yarn dyed with woad; black, grey or undyed natural-coloured yarn. The colour palette was quite limited. Madder, a plant from which a vermilion red dye can be extracted, was very expensive and was not used for ganseys, as it was in England. Along the Zuiderzee coast, cornflower-blue was the preferred colour. As a sign of mourning – and due to the nature of the profession, mourning a death in the family was very common – these cornflower-blue ganseys would be dyed black, usually resulting in a very dark blue. Knitters therefore decided to knit all ganseys in dark blue yarn, which saved them from having to dye them later. Cornflower-blue disappeared as a main colour, but it was still used now and then. The first synthetic dyes came onto the market around 1900.

Fishermen sometimes brought merino wool with them from England, which was of a good quality and widely available there. They also smuggled wool home from

58 BLUE AND BLACK SAGATHY FROM MUSEUM HET OUDE RAADHUIS, URK

Iceland. The Icelandic wool was firmer, because of the cold conditions the sheep were exposed to, and looked a lot like sagathy. Until after the Second World War, sagathy was not only used for knitting ganseys, but also for stockings, socks and underwear. At the beginning of the 1960s, sagathy disappeared because people felt it was a bit shabby-looking, coarse, scratchy and heavy. From then on, ganseys were knitted using sock yarn or synthetic yarn. The black sagathy that I received from some of the ladies during my visits and which I used to knit samples with, has a beautiful sheen and is not comparable to modern yarns. Frangipani Guernsey Wool from England and Loret Karman RAW yarn from the Netherlands (developed by Loret Karman according to an old recipe) come close; however, these otherwise beautiful yarns lack the special sheen that is so characteristic of the original sagathy (fig. 58). For sweaters that require frequent washing, cotton is recommended, or a good wool-acrylic or cotton-acrylic blend.

T-MODEL

The T-model of the ganseys was always knitted according to the same 'recipe': the chest circumference + 4–6cm (1½–2¼in). For children, 2–4cm (¾–1½in) or more was added to the chest circumference (depending on fashion and to take growth into account). The hems and cuffs were sometimes knitted with the yarn held double, to prevent wearing out too fast. Two-thirds of the total length was knitted, up to armhole height, on four or five thin double-pointed needles – much thinner than we would use now, to make the fabric as dense as possible – after which the work was divided in half and the front and back were knitted separately on two needles. The back was knitted as a rectangle, while the front was divided into three parts for the neckline and shoulders when you got to the hollow of the neck. The shoulders were then knitted up to the same height as the back, and the stitches of front and back were bound off together with a three-needle cast-off, either on the inside or outside. This would create the two armholes, one-third of the height of the entire sweater, with an opening large enough for the head (it is important to take good measurements, especially when knitting for small children, or to knit a placket or shoulder opening, because a child's head is proportionally larger than that of an adult), after which a ribbed collar was added. Stitches were then picked up around the armholes and the sleeves were knitted down, in the round and towards the wrist, gradually decreasing stitches. Sleeves were always knitted a bit too short, to keep the forearms and hands free for work. In order to protect the forearms during work, leather or oilskin sleeve protectors were worn.

YARN TYPES

It is still worthwhile to knit 100 per cent wool sweaters yourself. Store-bought pure wool sweaters are considerably more expensive than the wool you'd need to knit a sweater yourself. For very young children or if you are allergic to wool (or probably to low quality wool), you can use a good quality synthetic yarn, a blend or cotton yarn, but 100 per cent wool is preferred. Wool has excellent properties which no other fibre can top: it is a natural product, provides perfect ventilation, protects against the cold, stimulates the body's heat production, is water and dirt repellent and very elastic, so that it forms itself to the body and does not crease. There were no synthetic yarns in those days, but even now, they can't compete with 100 per cent wool. Synthetic yarns are more stuffy to wear, attract dirt and pill much more quickly, ruining your beautiful knitting.

To show the effect of different types of yarn and different needle sizes, the ganseys are knitted in different types of yarns and on different needles: from fine (2–2.5mm/UK 14–13/US 0–1) through regular (3–3.5mm/ UK 11–10/US 2–4) to thick needles (4–4.5mm/UK 8–7/ US 6–7). If you use even thicker yarn and thicker needles, the effect of repetitive motifs in a pattern gets lost in a small gansey. To make your choice easier, some samples of the same motif in different yarn thicknesses and colours, knitted on thinner and thicker needles, are shown in Motifs and Patterns (pages 48–50).

Yarn types and colours can be discontinued. In that case, look for an alternative by the same or a different brand, in yarn stores or on the Internet. Pay attention to the yardage per 50 or 100 grams (1¾ or 3½ ounces), the recommended needle size and the dye lot.

YARN FOR 2–3MM (UK 14–11/US 0–2) NEEDLES.

YARN FOR 2.5–4MM (UK 13–8/US 1–6) NEEDLES.

YARN FOR 3.5–5MM (UK 10–6/US 4–8) NEEDLES.

Thin or thick, firm or soft wool

You can find smooth wool, blends and synthetic yarns for any needle size. In this section, we limit ourselves to cotton, wool and some beautiful wool blend yarns.

For small children, choose a yarn that is easy to wash and that provides good ventilation and moisture regulation. Cotton and wool blend yarns with a good quality acrylic are suitable. Some types of wool will feel a bit coarse at first, but during knitting and wearing they become softer.

To solve this problem completely, you can put the gansey in cold water for 15 minutes with a bit of Eucalan or fabric softener. Do not rinse or wring out the gansey: gently squeeze out any excess water, roll up the gansey in a thick towel and leave to dry flat on another thick towel to avoid sagging. This will make the gansey a lot more comfortable to wear. Give your swatch the same treatment, so you can see and feel the effect, and calculate your stitch count.

AMOUNT OF YARN

The amount of yarn you need depends on the size of the gansey. The larger the size and the more motifs you use, the more yarn you will need. When using thicker yarn, you will need more balls or skeins than with thinner yarn. As a rule of thumb, a men's gansey size 48–50 (medium–large) in stocking (stockinette) stitch requires an average yardage of 1600–1700m (1750–1860yd); with patterns, this goes up to 1700–1800m (1860–1970yd). The yardage per ball or skein is specified on the ball band, and varies per type and brand: with some yarns, you will only need 500g (17⅝oz) or less, while you may need 800g (28¼oz) or more of another yarn. Always check the yardage, as it is a more reliable indication. Always knit a swatch (see page 47) first, to avoid ganseys that don't fit and other disappointments!

For a child's gansey, you will need 200–600g (7–21¼oz), or 500–1200m (550–1310yd). Always check if all the wool you need is from the same dye lot. Yarn has a colour number, accompanied by a second number for the dye lot. All numbers should match. **The quantities, needle sizes and tension (gauge) given for the ganseys in this book are based on the knitting of the individual knitters. They should be seen as a recommendation, and your knitting may be different!** It's better to buy some extra yarn; you can often return balls or skeins that are left over to the store, or use them for a matching hat or scarf.

TOOLS

Knitting needles are available in different materials: aluminium, steel, wood, bamboo and plastic. The lower the number, the thinner the needles; the higher the number, the thicker the needles (except UK needle sizes, where the reverse is true). Conversions are given for all needles to make it easy to select the correct ones. For flat knitting, use 40cm (15¾in) long straight knitting needles. For knitting in the round there are special circular needles, for example by KnitPro or Prym. You can also use four or five double-pointed knitting needles, but it's quite complicated if you've never done that before.

Handy tools and notions to have are a needle gauge, to check the thickness of the knitting needles; cable needles when knitting cables; stitch holders, or a piece of scrap yarn, to hold stitches that you will knit later; stitch markers to indicate the centre of a piece of knitting, or the start of a pattern repeat; a yarn buddy or bowl to prevent your ball from rolling away; a row counter to keep track of the number of rows or rounds knitted; a marking ruler to keep track of where you are in your chart; a knitting calculator to easily convert the number of stitches and rows for another needle size; a tape measure; darning needles; and a crochet hook to pick up dropped stitches or join flat knit pieces.

TECHNIQUES

Ganseys were always knitted in the round, so they have no seams, using four or five 2mm (UK 14/US 0) or 2.5mm (UK 13/US 1) double-pointed needles. The actual needle size, however, has never been indicated: there were copper needles and that is what you would knit with.

Knitting in the round

Knitting in the round is easy because you can knit most of the stitches and only have to purl for the motifs. The knitting charts in the book are based on knitting in the round. They show the front of the work, so you can easily see what the end result looks like and you can always check how the pattern is constructed (fig. 59).

59 GANSEY ON CIRCULAR NEEDLES

Knitting flat

Knitting flat is actually not a technique used for ganseys, but if you prefer, you can of course knit them flat. In your calculation of the number of stitches, take into account and add two edge stitches per piece, one on each side. You can only knit (V) the **odd rows** as indicated in the chart, so pay attention! The **even rows** must be knitted in reverse, or purled (–). So: V = –, – = V. You can always draw your own chart on squared paper if you're unsure about it.

SIZING

In the past, people would not use a pattern to knit garments, but a schematic lay-out: all sizes and stitches were divided into three, as described above (page 45). For a children's gansey, bear in mind that the head is relatively large. Always check whether they can pull the gansey over their head before you start knitting the collar! If not, adjust the neckline by making it deeper or wider. You can also knit a front placket, pick up more stitches for the neck than for the shoulders or leave one shoulder open and add a flap approximately 3cm (1¼in) onto the back left shoulder, with buttons, and add buttonholes in the top part of the same shoulder (cast off a few stitches, depending on the size of the buttons, and then cast on the same number of stitches in the next row).

Ganseys were worn with little to no ease. For a children's gansey with a bit more room, add 5–6cm (2–2¼in) to the chest circumference instead of 2–4cm (¾–1½cm), depending on what you or the child find pleasant and practical to wear.

An excellent way to determine the right size is to measure a sweater that fits well. In order to keep an eye on how you are progressing when you are knitting in the round, you can purl one stitch as a mock side seam, and weave in a length of yarn in a different colour to mark the centre of the front and back.

STITCHES USED

The stitches used for knitting ganseys are simple: variations of knit and purl stitches and cables. Knit stitches come forward when they are next to purled stitches, which appear more towards the background, while purl stitches above knit stitches come forward a bit. A stitch is wider than it is high. Therefore, you always need to knit more rows than the number of stitches you cast on to form a square. The only place where you need to increase and decrease is on the sleeves, unless you decide to knit a different type of armhole than the straight armhole used here. To knit other models, refer to a pattern from any knitting book. Knit the motifs according to the chart and follow the increases and decreases as stated in your pattern. Please note that your swatch has to match the tension (gauge) given in the knitting instructions; if necessary, use thicker or thinner yarn or thinner or thicker needles. Please note that cables can cause the knitted fabric to pull in a bit!

TENSION (GAUGE)

A swatch of at least 12 x 12cm (4¾ x 4¾in), knitted in the yarn and needles of your choice, incorporating all the motifs from the gansey you want to make, shows you what the motifs look like and whether you need to make adjustments (fig. 60). It helps to determine your tension (gauge) – the number of stitches and rows in a piece measuring 10 x 10cm (4 x 4in), which you can use to calculate the number of stitches you need to cast on and the number of rounds you need to knit to get the total height of your gansey, minus the hem. Divide the desired circumference of the gansey (actual chest circumference + 2–4cm (¾–1½in), see page 44) by 10 and multiply the result by the number of stitches in your 10 x 10cm (4 x 4in) swatch: this gives you the total number of stitches to cast on when you are knitting in the round. If your swatch gives you a tension of 20 sts per 10cm (4in), and the circumference of the gansey needs to be, for example, 104cm (50in), calculate 104/10 = 10.4 x 20 = 208 sts. If your tension is 21 stitches: 104/10 = 10.4 x 21 = 218.4 sts. Round it down to 218 sts, or up or down to the closest multiple of your motif, if necessary. Going back to the first example, if your motif is 6 sts wide, 208/6 = 34.67 motifs. Round this up to 35 motifs = 35 x 6 = 210 sts. Do the same for 218 sts, namely 218/6 = 36.33. 36 x 6 = 216 sts. The same applies to the number of rows: 28 rows = 10cm (4in). The height from hem to armhole, for example, is 38cm (15in). Your motif is 8 rows high; 28/8 = 3.5 motifs per 10cm (4in). 38/10 = 3.8 x 3.5= 13.3 motifs. This can be rounded down to 13 motifs (for a shorter gansey) or up to 14 motifs (for a longer gansey) before dividing the work for the armholes.

Make these calculations yourself a number of times based on your swatch and tension to get the hang of it. Practice makes perfect!

If you knit the front, back and sleeves separately, divide the total number of stitches needed by 2 and add 2 side stitches per pieces. Make the same calculations for the sleeves. Divide the desired length by 10cm (4in) and multiply by the number of rows per

10cm (4in). Look at the chart to see how many stitches and rows the motif you have chosen has, and adjust your stitch and row count accordingly, making sure the motif is centred on the front and back and also on the sleeve.

Make changes to the motif/pattern if necessary: for example, instead of 4 cables and 3 ladders, knit 5 cables and 4 ladders, or 3 cables and 2 ladders; instead of 2 purl stitches between the cables, do 1 purl stitch; instead of a 3-stitch cable, knit a 2-stitch cable; work more or less repeats of the motif; make the motif narrower or wider, for example, work a box over 4 stitches instead of 5 stitches; a diamond over 13 or 15 stitches instead of 11 stitches; make k2, p1 ribbing narrower by working k1, p1, etc. You can do whatever you want. Feel free to change a pattern if it suits you better – the fisherwomen did exactly the same!

Abbreviations	Purl 3 together: p3tog
Stitch(es): st(s)	Edge st: est
Knit stitch: k	Cable to the right: RC
Purl stitch: p	Cable to the left: LC

MOTIFS AND PATTERNS

A motif is the smallest independent part of a pattern, width- and height-wise. If you repeat a motif over and over again, this is called a pattern. Because of the dangers and hardships faced by fishermen at sea, they and their wives attached great value to symbolism. This can be seen in the motifs and patterns incorporated in the ganseys. They were derived from religion, the weather, the sea, the beach, the ship, fishing, fish and daily life. All motifs are knitted in countless variations, according to what people liked themselves; there are no 100 per cent fixed motifs and patterns for ganseys. The motifs and patterns in these charts are only guidelines, indications and interpretations.

If you want to make a pattern bigger or smaller, you can do so by knitting it on thicker needles and with thicker wool (larger) or on thinner needles and with thinner wool (smaller) or by adjusting it as you wish. If you want to combine other motifs than those described for a gansey, you are free to do so. Feel free to give your sweater your own personal twist.

Lightning bolts (weather)
Lightning on land is awe-inspiring, but it is nothing compared to thunderstorms at sea.

Squares (fishing, buildings)
Squares symbolize both the nets used by fishermen and the bricks in the houses.

Boxes in ganseys from Arnemuiden and Zandvoort.

Boxes in ganseys from Marken, Brouwershaven and Durgerdam.

Boxes in ganseys from Stellendam and Paesens-Moddergat.

Tides (sea)
The alternate use of horizontal bands of stocking (stockinette) stitch and motifs is called low and high tide.

Eye of God, flower or diamond (religion)
The all-seeing eye of God is a centuries-old motif already used in the ancient world, and is found in countless cultures. The motif is also called the flower, or diamond, as a symbol of prosperity. It provided protection and security, but in the eyes of the women also ensured the fisherman remained faithful when travelling to foreign ports. Machine-knitted English sweaters were knitted in smooth stocking (stockinette) stitch, with an Eye of God on the chest in lace stitches, consisting of a large diamond in the centre and four smaller diamonds on each point.

Waves (sea)

Waves are an unavoidable element at sea and, in combination with strong winds, can be very dangerous.

Hailstones (weather)

Hailstones are represented by moss stitch and variations of this stitch.

Cable (religion and ship)

Cables stand for something to hold on to, and on Urk, for example, they represent a closeness to God. The ropes used to hoist the sails and moor the ship at the quay are symbolized in all kinds of different cables.

Chain (ship)

A chain was needed to attach the anchor. Chains can be a variation on a cable pattern, but are also knit as staggered horizontal purled stripes.

Ladder or Jacob's ladder (religion and ship)

On the high seas, a rope ladder was necessary to get from the boat into a sloop, and vice versa. Again on Urk they symbolized closeness to God. Ladders can be knitted with different spacings in between.

Tree of life (daily life)

The tree of life symbolizes parentage from father to son. This family tree does not include the mothers and daughters, they were a separate unit. The tree of life resembles the herringbone motif, but the branches are closer together.

Arrows (fishing)

Arrows or harpoons were indispensable when trying to catch, kill and bring in large fish.

Ridges (beach)

Horizontal and slanted garter stitch ridges represent sandy ridges on the beach.

Diamonds (fishing, religion)

Diamonds are knitted in many variations; the eye of God and nets also have a diamond shape.

Herringbone (fish)

The herringbone motif is used both horizontally and vertically.

Fishing nets (fishing)

All variations of continuous, linked diamonds are inspired by the nets the fishermen used.

Flags (fishing)

Flags were very important for communication at sea. The number and way in which flags were raised had a clear meaning. With flags, a ship was able to communicate whether it had had a good catch, or a bad one, that it was in trouble, and more. This idea is the basis of the annual *Vlaggetjesdag* (Flag Day) celebrations, when all fishing vessels were on show in the port, flags blowing in the wind.

Rigging (ship)

Rigging comprises all the ropes and ties on a ship. It is represented in knitting as a combination of cables and vertical motifs and used in the upper part of ganseys.

BASIC SIZES

For the basic sweater sizes, add 2–4cm (¾–1¼in) if you are knitting in the round, 1–2cm (½–¾in) per piece when knitting flat, to the total chest circumference (see 'A' in the sketch opposite). Adjust the sizes based on the measured chest circumference if you want more or less ease, or if you want to knit the gansey bit bigger so the child can wear it for longer. Determine the length of the body from hem to armholes: you can make the sweater longer or shorter than indicated here. The armhole height is approximately a third of the total sweater height, or as high as you feel is comfortable, based on the circumference of the thickest part of the upper arm. Divide the top for the neckline and shoulders on the basis of half the chest circumference + ease. Always allow a bit more room for the neckline than for the shoulders. Measure the neckline depth from the shoulders down to the hollow of the neck. A child's head is much larger compared to an adult's head. Always allow for a wider opening, make the neckline slightly deeper, knit a placket or keep one shoulder open, to close with buttons. If you have a sweater that fits well, use it for your measurements! Measure the sleeve length from the armpit to the wrist, letting the arm hang against the body. **The sizes given here are standard sizes which can easily be customized based on your actual sizes and preferences!** Because all models are the same and the chest circumference is the starting point, the instructions apply to both boys' and girls' sweaters.

Age	1	2	3	4	5	6	7	8	9	10	11	12	13	14
Size/Height – cm	86	92	98	104	110	116	122	128	134	140	146	152	158	164
– ft + in	2ft 10"	3ft ¼"	3ft 2¼"	3ft 5"	3ft 7¾"	3ft 9¾"	4ft	4ft 2½"	4ft 4¾"	4ft 7"	4ft 9½"	4ft 11¾"	5ft 2¼"	5ft 4½"
(A) Chest circumference	49cm	52	53	55	56	58	60	62	63	66	71	75	80	86
	19¼in	20½	21	21⅝	22	23	23⅝	24½	24¾	26	28	29½	31½	33¾
(B) Height up to armhole (excl. hem)	20cm	21	23	25	26	28	29	30	31	32	33	34	36	39
	8in	8¼	9	9¾	10¼	11	11½	12	12¼	12½	13	13⅜	14¼	15¼
(C) Armhole height	11cm	12	12	13	14	14	15	15	16	16	17	17	18	18
	4¼in	4¾	4¾	5	5½	5½	6	6	6¼	6¼	6¾	6¾	7	7
(D) Sleeve length up to forearm (excl. cuff)	22cm	23	25	27	28	30	32	34	35	36	37	38	39	39
	8⅝in	9	9¾	10⅜	11	11¾	12½	13⅜	13¾	14	14½	15	15¼	15¼
(E) Total wrist circumference	14cm	16	18	18	18	19	19	19	20	20	20	21	21	21
	5½in	6¼	7	7	7	7½	7½	7½	8	8	8	8¼	8¼	8¼

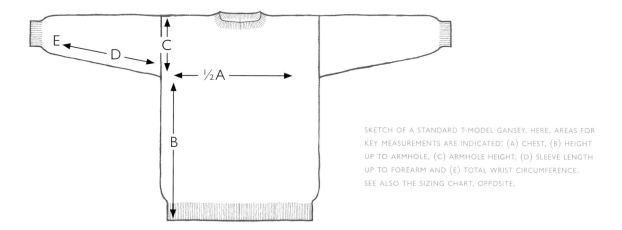

CHART AND SKETCH

Within each knitting pattern, the part or parts of a chart or diagram forming the basic motif or motifs are marked in a lighter blue colour. Furthermore, the numbers of the stitches (below the chart) and rows or rounds (to the right of the chart) of the motif are also marked with corresponding colours. The centre-front is marked in red (see Chart Key). If a motif is very large, it sometimes has to be repeated in mirror image from the centre-front stitch. Refer to the sketch of the gansey design (such as the one above) for more information. Cables are sometimes the same throughout the entire pattern, all crossing to the left or to the right, but sometimes they are knitted in the opposite direction on the other side of the centre-front/back. If you want a motif to line up exactly in the middle, start counting it out from the centre-front stitch to the right, to determine what stitch to start with, based on your swatch and the number of stitches you cast on. If the motif and pattern do not fit nicely, you can add or subtract one or more stitches from the total and add or subtract a pattern repeat, or simply work the extra stitches under the armpits (at the beginning and end of a piece when knitting flat) in plain stocking (stockinette) stitch, or in a stitch pattern that matches the motif. Make a swatch if you don't fully trust your counting capabilities or copy the chart a number of times, so you can see in advance how a design will turn out and if you should adjust it. This will cost you less time than knitting a gansey that isn't put together properly!

Each motif consists of a certain number of stitches and rows, which are repeated as often as necessary. If you knit in the round you can follow the chart exactly. If you knit flat, make sure that you purl all knit stitches (V) and knit all purl stitches (–) on the return row. Preferably the number of stitches you cast on is a multiple of the number of stitches in the motif. Each chart shows a few repeats of the motif used, so that you can see the effect of repeating the motif. *This does not mean that these are the only repeats of stitches and rows:* often, there are considerably more, depending on the width and height of the sweater, and which part of the sweater contains the pattern to be knitted; you can refer to the sketch for more information.

Chart Key

V = knit

– = purl

= cable to the right

= cable to the left

= knit 2 together, yarn-over, yarn-over, knit 2 together: 1 lace hole

= yarn-over, knit 3 together, yarn-over: 2 lace holes

= centre front   = sixth motif

= first motif   = seventh motif

= second motif   = eighth motif

= third motif   = ninth motif

= fourth motif   = tenth motif

= fifth motif   = eleventh motif

= twelfth motif

GENERAL KNITTING INSTRUCTIONS

The general instructions for a gansey are based on wool suitable for 3mm (UK 11/US 2) and 3.5mm (UK 10/US 4) needles. If you knit on thinner or thicker needles, or have chosen a narrower or wider motif, you have to base your calculations on your swatch and the chosen motif!

KNITTING IN THE ROUND

Take the measurements of the person for whom you are knitting the gansey, or measure a well-fitting sweater. Check the chart and sketch for the sweater you want to knit for the placement of the motifs and to see if the motif (or for example cables) are knitted the same all over or whether they should be mirrored. Start by knitting a swatch, both in stocking (stockinette) stitch and in the chosen motif. Block your swatch, slightly stretching it using stainless steel pins, between damp towels and let it dry naturally. After blocking, measure the number of stitches and rows in 10 x

10cm (4 x 4in) to determine your tension (gauge) (fig. 61). Now calculate the number of stitches for the basic motif or motifs that form the pattern. Use your tension (gauge) as the base for your calculation. Refer to the sketch to see how wide each pattern should be and determine the number of repeats of a basic motif you need to knit per round or per pattern section. Now calculate how many stitches you need to cast on in total.

Body front and back

Choose the desired size and, based on your swatch and tension (gauge), cast on the required number of stitches – a multiple of the number of stitches required for the chosen motif – on circular needles (3mm/UK 11/US 2). Knit a 3–5cm (1¼–2in) hem in ribbing. Change to larger needles (3.5mm/UK 10/US 4) and work in stocking (stockinette) stitch (knit all stitches) up to where the pattern begins, or start knitting the chosen pattern immediately, following the chart for the relevant gansey. If necessary, you can increase the number of stitches after the ribbing to make the pattern fit. If the pattern contains a lot of cables, increase approximately 10–14 stitches distributed evenly where the cables start as cables can pull in your work! This means you may have to increase stitches for the cables right above the ribbing or higher up, if you are only knitting cables on the top part. Use a stitch marker or safety pin to indicate the start of a row or round, the centre-front and the 'side seams'. Knit up to the armholes. Divide the work into two equal parts for the front and back. The pieces are now knitted separately and flat, using straight knitting needles (or circular needles, if you prefer), up to the neckline. Please note: the chart can now be followed only for the odd (right side) rows. All even (wrong side) rows, need to be worked the other way round: every knit stitch (V) is now a purl stitch, every purl stitch (–) should be a knit stitch. For the neckline, put a bit more than one third of the stitches in the centre on a stitch holder or piece of scrap yarn (see size chart on page 50). For the front piece, continue 3–5cm (1¼–2in) for both shoulders (for a rounder neckline, cast off a few stitches on the neckline sides) and then place these stitches on hold. Continue knitting the back piece up to the desired height. Close the shoulder seams as follows: knit together 1 stitch from the front and 1 stitch from the back. Do the same again and then pass over the first stitch. Continue knitting together and casting off all stitches. Close both shoulders in this manner, either on the outside, to create a visible seam, or on the inside. Put the remaining stitches of the back piece for the neckline on a stitch holder or spare needle.

Collar

Put all held stitches on thinner circular needles (3mm/UK 11/US 2) in this example) and pick up stitches along the edges on the front neckline. Make sure the opening is big enough for the head (try it on before moving on to the sleeves) and if necessary, pick up a few more stitches to prevent holes. It's better to pick up some extra stitches, especially on the sides, for example by knitting 2 stitches in 1 edge stitch, which you can then knit together in the next row. Knit 4cm (1½in) or more in ribbing. Cast off loosely.

Sleeves

Multiply the required length for the sleeves + approximately 1–2cm (½–¾in) extra length by your row tension (gauge) per 1cm (½in) to calculate how many rounds you need to knit in pattern from the armhole to the cuff. Count how many stitches you are starting with and how many stitches you should have left over based on the desired wrist circumference. Divide the number of rounds to knit by the difference between the two numbers. The resulting number tells you how often and after how many rounds you have to decrease stitches. For example: you start with 74 sts at the armhole and want to end with 54 sts after 140 rounds. This means that you have to decrease 20 sts over the length of the sleeve. When knitting in the round, to avoid warping, alternately decrease to the left and right of the middle stitch at the underside of the sleeve; in this case every 7 rounds. With knitting flat, decrease 1 st at the start and the end of the row every 14 rows. For the sleeves, pick up stitches in the edge stitches of the armhole on 40cm (15¾in) circular needles (3.5mm/UK 10/US 4). On the first row or round, distributed over the entire circumference of the sleeve, knit 2 stitches in each edge stitch, and then knit together as many stitches as needed in the second row or round until you have the number of stitches you need.

Distribute the decreases evenly. Make sure that the total number of stitches is a multiple of the width of your chosen motif. When you get to the cuff, change to the thinner needles (3mm/UK 11/US 2) and knit 3–5cm (1¼–2in) of ribbing. Cast off loosely. Sometimes a gansey becomes too heavy when you knit the sleeves directly into the armholes. You can also knit them separately, casting on the number of stitches you need to fill the armhole and ending with the cuff. The sleeves can then be sewn into the armholes (invisibly by using mattress stitch).

Finishing

Weave in any ends with a darning needle. If you used quite a coarse type of yarn, soak your gansey in water with a dash of Eucalan. Do not rinse, gently press out the excess water and leave to dry flat on a towel. You can lightly block your gansey between two damp towels and leave to dry (also see fig. 61, page 51), to smooth out your knitting. You can also put the gansey under a cloth and steam with a steam iron on a fairly high setting, without touching the cloth. Do not iron, as this can flatten raised stitches and cables. If you treat your ganseys well, they will look and feel amazing.

FLAT KNITTING

Choose the desired size and cast on the number of stitches for the back or front piece, which should be a multiple of the number of stitches you need based on the tension (gauge) and the chosen motif + 2 side stitches (also see Tension (Gauge), page 47). Please note: the chart can only be followed for the odd (right side) rows. All even (wrong side) rows, need to be knitted the other way round: every knit stitch (V) is now a purl stitch, every purl stitch (–) should be a knit stitch!

GENERAL INFORMATION

No extensive knitting instructions are given for the ganseys. However, each gansey pattern includes a sketch, a chart based on the old photographs, size information and a list of materials. **Always use the general instructions on page 51.** Where necessary, write down the alterations or adjustments you are making to the gansey for later reference. **Always adjust the sizes, stitch count and row count on the basis of your tension (gauge).**

6 NORTH SEA COAST

SCHOT, THE MUSSELS BEING UNLOADED, THOLEN, CA. 1920

Herring fishing on the North Sea was of vital importance to the Netherlands, and led to the wearing of ganseys as a result of contact with English and Scottish fishermen who already fished there. Fish boosted the nation economically in the seventeenth century: at the time, the export of herring brought in more money than the maritime trade with the East Indies. In the heyday of the ganseys, between 1870–1950, herring was as important for the economy as it was for feeding the people. In addition, longline fishing for haddock and cod on the seas around Iceland was of great importance, as was fishing for flatfish, shrimp and mussels close to shore.

Fishermen from the coastal towns on De Zijde, the area between Den Helder and Hoek van Holland, sailed with *bomschuiten* (flat-bottomed vessels) from the beach out to sea, and luggers and longliners would be moored in the ports of Vlaardingen, Pernis, Maassluis, Zwartewaal, Middelharnis, etc. In the waters of Zeeland, they fished with *hengsten*, *snikken*, *hoogaarzen* and *aken* (all types of barges).

Ganseys from towns on the North Sea coast are very varied: from sober in Zeeland – under the influence of Calvinist religion and poverty – to richly patterned on the South Holland islands, and on De Zijde, ganseys were often stocking (stockinette) stitch up to the chest with stocking (stockinette) stitch sleeves. Many variations of the patterns were found, combined with patterns from other areas, as women would knit what they liked and also wanted to distinguish themselves.

NORTH HOLLAND
DEN HELDER/ HUISDUINEN

The towns of Huisduinen and Den Helder were located on the island of Huisduinen. A deed from 1775 shows that both villages were lost to the sea after the All Saints' Flood of 1570 and they were rebuilt further inland on the island. In 1610, a sand dike was built between Huisduinen and Callantsoog, so the island was no longer an island. In 1819, the excavation of the Great North Holland Canal was started with the aim of providing Amsterdam, which threatened to lose its connection with the sea due to the silting up of Pampus, with a good seaway. This made Den Helder a prosperous town. However, in 1878 the much shorter North Sea Canal between Amsterdam and IJmuiden was completed, ending the period of growth and boom for the town. Only the navy and the government shipyard remained in Den Helder.

Den Helder and fishing are inextricably linked. In 1900, the fishing fleet of Den Helder consisted of thirty-four *botters*, thirteen *schokkers*, sixteen *blazers*, four *kotters*, eight *barges*, one *stoomblazer*, one yacht (*jacht*) and 135 *vletten*. The proceeds of the fish auction in that year amounted to 379,444.35 krone. In comparison, in 1975, the annual turnover was 54,018,634.62 krone. In 1906, an additional fish auction and shelter were built near the Wierhoofd, for use in bad weather, mainly for the sale of the herring catch. This Zuiderzee herring was brought in by herring pullers, the *haringtrekkers*, who would pull the catch, caught with trawling and drift nets, up to the beach and the sandbanks near Huisduinen and Texel, walking in the sea with their long trousers, called *hozen*. Herring, anchovies and garfish migrated to the Zuiderzee to spawn via the Marsdiep. The construction of the Afsluitdijk dam and causeway in 1932 put an end to this custom.

Many different ganseys were found in Den Helder with various types of squares, but also sideways-knitted ganseys and ganseys with the Eye of God motif, possibly influenced by the Urker fishermen who settled in Den Helder before 1900.

63 HERRING PULLERS ON THE BEACH AT HUISDUINEN, CA. 1910. KNRM ARCHIVE, DEN HELDER
64 FISHERMEN ON THE BEACH AT HUISDUINEN, CA. 1900. KNRM ARCHIVE, DEN HELDER

DEN HELDER 7 GANSEY

AGE: 7–8 YEARS (SIZE: 128CM/4FT 2½IN), CHEST CIRCUMFERENCE: 62CM (24½IN) + 4CM (1½IN) = 66CM (26IN), TOTAL HEIGHT: 47CM (18½IN)

Knit a swatch first, with different sized needles if necessary. A gansey should not be too loosely knitted. Follow the chart for the motif and adjust the width and/or height to your size, the yarn used and your tension (gauge). Follow the general instructions for knitting ganseys on page 51 and adjust where necessary.

Measurements

WIDTH: 2 x 33cm (13in) = 66cm (26in)

SHOULDERS: 10cm (4in)

NECK: 13cm (5¼in)

NECKLINE DEPTH: 3–4cm (1¼–1½in)

ARMHOLE HEIGHT: 15–16cm (6–6¼in)

HEIGHT UP TO ARMHOLE, EXCL. RIBBING: 30cm (11¾in)

SLEEVE LENGTH, EXCL. RIBBING: 32cm (12½in)

WRIST CIRCUMFERENCE: approx. 19cm (7½in)

RIBBING: 3–4cm (1¼–1½in), as preferred

Materials

∞ 6–7 balls of De Rerum Natura Ulysse 5-ply in Sel, or equivalent 5-ply (sport) yarn in cream; 50g/202yd/185m

∞ 2mm (UK 14/US 0) and 2.5mm (UK 13/US 1) circular needles

∞ 2.5mm (UK 13/US 1) straight needles

∞ 4 buttons

TENSION (GAUGE): 27 sts x 45 rows on 2.5mm (UK 13/US 1) needles = 10 x 10cm (4 x 4in)

RIBBING: k2, p2

DETAIL OF A YOUNG FISHERMAN FROM FIG. 64, OPPOSITE

NORTH HOLLAND
EGMOND AAN ZEE

In the sixteenth century, Egmond was the most important fishing village on De Zijde, where fishermen with flat-bottomed vessels such as the Egmonder *pinck* and later the *bomschuit* went out to sea from the beach. Around 1900, when the *bomschuiten* were no longer used, many Egmonders moved to IJmuiden to work on steam trawlers and luggers and settled there.

Egmond aan Zee was isolated from the outside world for many centuries. The only way to get there was along a dirt track. In 1847, the situation improved a lot when the Egmonderstraatweg highway was built, followed by a small railway line to Alkmaar in 1905. The steam tram brought workmen to the city, and also brought more tourists to Egmond every year. On old postcards you can still see that this was a time of elegant hotels and guesthouses and bathing machines on the beach. In the crisis years things went so badly that the tram was closed in 1934.

With every storm flood, a part of the village would disappear into the sea. The Boulevard, which now runs along the sea, once ran through the village. There was also a lot of coastal erosion in 1905, in 1976 and again in 1990. Sand nourishment now ensures that the beach and the Boulevard are preserved. After a storm, at low tide you can still sometimes find shards and stones of the lost Egmond.

Like most ganseys from towns on De Zijde, the ganseys in Egmond only had motifs on the chest area.

65 THE LAST *BOMSCHUITEN* ON THE BEACH AT EGMOND AAN ZEE, 1895
66 PHOTO TAKEN AS PART OF RESEARCH INTO TRADITIONAL COSTUMES IN THE NETHERLANDS AROUND 1910. MOTHER AND SON IN A GANSEY FROM EGMOND. HISTORISCH EGMOND
DETAIL OF YOUNG BOY WEARING EGMOND 4 GANSEY, FROM FIG. 66, LEFT

TYPE. EGMOND a ZEE.

STRAND EGMOND AAN ZEE.

EGMOND 4 GANSEY

AGE: 7–8 YEARS (SIZE: 128CM/4FT 2½IN), CHEST CIRCUMFERENCE: 62CM (24½IN) + 4CM (1½IN) = 66CM (26IN), TOTAL HEIGHT: 47CM (18½IN)

Knit a swatch first, with different sized needles if necessary. A gansey should not be too loosely knitted. Follow the chart for the motif and adjust the width and/or height to your size, the yarn used and your tension (gauge). Follow the general instructions for knitting ganseys on page 51 and adjust where necessary.

Measurements

WIDTH: 2 x 33cm (13in) = 66cm (26in)

SHOULDERS: 10cm (4in)

NECK: 13cm (5¼in)

NECKLINE DEPTH: 3–4cm (1¼–1½in)

ARMHOLE HEIGHT: 15–16 cm (6–6¼in)

HEIGHT UP TO ARMHOLE, EXCL. RIBBING:
   30cm (11¾in)

SLEEVE LENGTH, EXCL. RIBBING: 32cm (12½in)

WRIST CIRCUMFERENCE: approx. 19cm (7½in)

RIBBING: 3–4cm (1¼–1½in), as preferred

Materials

∞ 8 balls SMC Extra Soft Merino in 5402, or equivalent DK (light worsted/8-ply) yarn in navy blue; 50g/142yd/130m

∞ 2.75mm (UK 12/US 2) and 3mm (UK 11/US 2) circular needles

∞ 3mm (UK 11/US 2) straight needles

∞ cable needle

TENSION (GAUGE): 25 sts x 33 rows on 3mm (UK 11/US 2) needles = 10 x 10cm (4 x 4in)

RIBBING: k1, p1

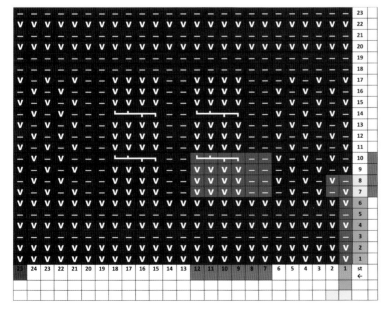

NORTH HOLLAND
ZANDVOORT

Every day fishermen went out to sea to catch plaice and cod, first with *pincken* then, from the middle of the eighteenth century, they used slightly larger *bomschuiten* – both flat-bottomed barges. Until well into the nineteenth century, you could see heavily loaded fish peddlers – men and women – barefoot or in stockings, walking along the sandy Fisherman's Path to the Kraantje Lek inn. There they put on their clogs to walk to the Fish Hall in the Grote Markt in Haarlem. Later, the tram line was built parallel to the Fisherman's Path.

In the nineteenth and twentieth centuries, Zandvoort developed from a fishing village into a popular seaside resort. More and more fishermen left the profession and slowly but surely fishing disappeared from Zandvoort. The remaining fishermen moved to IJmuiden, because it had a port and a fish market. You could then immediately sell your catch, instead of having to walk all the way to Haarlem!

In Zandvoort, we found stocking (stockinette) stitch ganseys with a patterned yoke as well as ganseys with a continuous motif and a centre band.

67 YOUNG FISHERMAN FROM ZANDVOORT IN THE GROTE HOUTSTRAAT IN HAARLEM.
NORTH HOLLAND ARCHIVE

THE ZANDVOORT 1 GANSEY CAN BE FOUND ON PAGES 58–60 OF *DUTCH TRADITIONAL GANSEYS*;
2 CAN BE FOUND ON PAGE 71 OF *MORE TRADITIONAL DUTCH GANSEYS*.

ZANDVOORT 3 GANSEY

AGE: 12–13 YEARS (SIZE: 158CM/5FT 2¼IN), CHEST CIRCUMFERENCE:
80CM (31½IN) + 4CM (1½IN) = 84CM (33IN), TOTAL HEIGHT: 58CM
(22¾IN)

*Knit a swatch first, with different sized needles if necessary. A gansey should not be
too loosely knitted. Follow the chart for the motif and adjust the width and/or height
to your size, the yarn used and your tension (gauge). Follow the general instructions for
knitting ganseys on page 51 and adjust where necessary.*

Measurements

WIDTH: 2 x 42cm (16½in) = 84cm (33in)

SHOULDERS: 13.5cm (5¼in)

NECK: 15cm (6in)

NECKLINE DEPTH: 4–5cm (1½–2in)

ARMHOLE HEIGHT: 18cm (7in)

HEIGHT UP TO ARMHOLE, EXCL. RIBBING: 36cm (14¼in)

SLEEVE LENGTH, EXCL. RIBBING: 38cm (15in)

WRIST CIRCUMFERENCE: approx. 21cm (8¼in)

RIBBING: 4–5cm (1½–2in), as preferred

Materials

∞ 13 balls Lang Thema Nuova in 0035, or
equivalent 5-ply (sport) yarn in medium blue;
50g/129yd/118m

∞ 3mm (UK 11/US 2) and 3.5mm (UK 10/US 4)
circular needles

∞ 3.5mm (UK 10/US 4) straight needles

∞ 4 buttons

TENSION (GAUGE): 23 sts x 32 rows on 3.5mm
(UK 10/US 4) needles = 10 x 10cm (4 x 4in)

RIBBING: k1, p1

68 THEATRE COMPANY DE WURF FROM ZANDVOORT PERFORMS IN
TRADITIONAL CLOTHING, INCLUDING A GANSEY THAT STRONGLY
RESEMBLES THE CHILDREN'S GANSEY IN FIG. 67. ZANDVOORT VROEGER

SOUTH HOLLAND
NOORDWIJK

The name Noordwijk is mentioned for the first time as 'Nortich' in a document from the ninth century. However, the area was already inhabited well before this. The location on the North Sea was especially decisive for the character and development of the town. In 1429, the bishop of Utrecht gave Noordwijk the status of a place of pilgrimage because Saint Jerome, a Scottish monk, was reportedly tortured to death there in 857. The local church was dedicated to Saint Jerome (*Jeroen* in Dutch). Many Noordwijkers worked in agriculture and husbandry, but sea fishing with *pincken* and *bomschuiten* created related industries such as smokehouses, shipyards and tanning shops, which employed many residents. The most important market for fresh fish was nearby Leiden. The last *bomschuit* disappeared around 1900, and the fashionable seaside resort of Noordwijk remained.

The Noordwijk gansey is known for its bramble stitch. The motif seems to come from Denmark, but this cannot be proven.

71 NOORDWIJK IN 1908. JAN WILLEMSEN

NOORDWIJK GANSEY

AGE: 11–12 YEARS (SIZE: 152CM/4FT 11¼IN), CHEST CIRCUMFERENCE: 76CM (30IN) + 4CM (1½IN) = 80CM (31½IN), TOTAL HEIGHT: 55CM (21¾IN)

Bramble stitch is used for the motif bands in the Noordwijk gansey. The bands in between are knitted in stocking (stockinette) stitch. Knit a swatch first, with different sized needles if necessary. A gansey should not be too loosely knitted. Follow the chart for the motif and adjust the width and/or height to your size, the yarn used and your tension (gauge). Follow the general instructions for knitting ganseys on page 51 and adjust where necessary.

Measurements

WIDTH: 2 x 40cm (15¾in) = 80cm (31½in)

SHOULDERS: 13cm (5¼in)

NECK: 14cm (5½in)

NECKLINE DEPTH: 3–4cm (1¼–1½in)

ARMHOLE HEIGHT: 17cm (6¾in)

HEIGHT UP TO ARMHOLE, EXCL. RIBBING: approx. 34cm (13½in)

SLEEVE LENGTH, EXCL. RIBBING: 36cm (14¼in)

WRIST CIRCUMFERENCE: approx. 20cm (8in)

RIBBING: 3–5cm (1¼–2in), as preferred

Materials

∞ 5 balls Scheepjes Zuiderzee in 2, or equivalent aran (worsted/10-ply) yarn in cornflower blue; 100g/218yd/199m

∞ 4mm (UK 8/US 6) and 4.5mm (UK 7/US 7) circular needles

∞ 4.5mm (UK 7/US 7) straight needles

TENSION (GAUGE): 19 sts x 24 rows on 4.5mm (UK 7/US 7) needles = 10 x 10cm (4 x 4in)

RIBBING: k1, p1

BRAMBLE STITCH

Row 1: p1, *(k1, p1, k1) in next st, p3tog*, repeat from * to * until the end of the row.

Row 2: purl.

Row 3: *p3tog, (k1, p1, k1) in next st*, repeat from * to * until last stitch, p1.

Row 4: as row 2.

HAT

Choose an appealing tam hat and knit it using the bramble stitch. It is easiest if you choose a pattern with a multiple of 4 stitches + 1.

Fishing was and still is an important source of income for Katwijk. The fishermen first fished for fresh fish just along the coast using *bomschuiten*. The fish were then transported on foot by fisherwomen to Leiden and peddled there, but when the gutting ban was lifted in 1857 part of the fleet took those same *bomschuiten* further out to sea to fish for herring off the English east coast. However, the small crew of about seven people and unwieldy construction made them less suitable for this purpose.

When the much slimmer and faster lugger was introduced in 1866, Katwijk soon made the switch.

Because of their keel, luggers could not be landed on the beach, and Katwijk did not have a port. The Katwijk lugger fleet therefore chose the large port of Vlaardingen, then later in 1896 moved to the newly built port of IJmuiden.

In pictures, you regularly see Katwijkers wearing a Vlaardingen gansey, which might have been knitted for them there (fig. 72, 74) or by the Katwijk women who were inspired by the Vlaardingen designs. We found many different ganseys in Katwijk, seen in these school photographs. The Katwijk cable pullover is considered the most important.

SOUTH HOLLAND
KATWIJK

73 PRINS HENDRIKKANAAL IN KATWIJK, CA. 1912
(WITH THE KW 37 *AMICITIA*). KATWIJKS MUSEUM

THE KATWIJK 1 AND 2 GANSEYS CAN BE FOUND ON PAGES 66–68 OF *DUTCH TRADITIONAL GANSEYS*; 3–5 CAN BE FOUND ON PAGES 74–76 OF *MORE TRADITIONAL DUTCH GANSEYS*.

KATWIJK 2 GANSEY

AGE: 10–11 YEARS (SIZE: 146CM/4FT 9½IN), CHEST CIRCUMFERENCE: 71CM (28IN) + 3CM (1½IN) = 74CM (29¼IN), TOTAL HEIGHT: 56CM (22IN)

Knit a swatch first, with different sized needles if necessary. A gansey should not be too loosely knitted. Follow the chart for the motif and adjust the width and/or height to your size, the yarn used and your tension (gauge). Follow the general instructions for knitting ganseys on page 51 and adjust where necessary.

Measurements

WIDTH: 2 x 37cm (14½in) = 74cm (29¼in)

SHOULDERS: 11.5cm (4½in)

NECK: 14cm (5½in)

NECKLINE DEPTH: 3–4cm (1¼–1½in)

ARMHOLE HEIGHT: 17cm (6¾in)

HEIGHT UP TO ARMHOLE, EXCL. RIBBING: 33cm (13in)

SLEEVE LENGTH, EXCL. RIBBING: 38cm (15in)

WRIST CIRCUMFERENCE: approx. 20cm (8in)

RIBBING: 4–5cm (1½–2in), as preferred

Materials

∞ 7 balls Hjertegarn Vital in 6500 dark blue, or equivalent DK (light worsted/8-ply) yarn in dark blue; 50g/126yd/115m

∞ 3.5mm (UK 10/US 4) and 4mm (UK 8/US 6) circular needles

∞ 4mm (UK 8/US 6) straight needles

TENSION (GAUGE): 16 sts x 23 rows on 4mm (UK 8/US 6) needles = 10 x 10cm (4 x 4in)

RIBBING: k1, p1

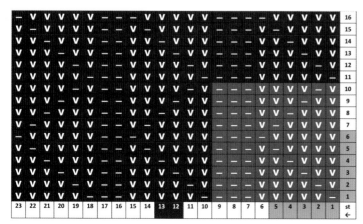

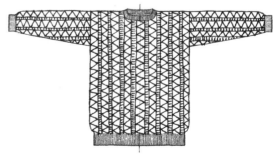

KATWIJK 6 GANSEY

AGE: 13–14 YEARS (SIZE: 164CM/5FT 4½IN), CHEST CIRCUMFERENCE: 84CM (33IN) + 4CM (1½IN) = 88CM (34¾IN), TOTAL HEIGHT: 56–58CM (22–22¾IN)

Knit a swatch first, with different sized needles if necessary. A gansey should not be too loosely knitted. Follow the chart for the motif and adjust the width and/or height to your size, the yarn used and your tension (gauge). Follow the general instructions for knitting ganseys on page 51 and adjust where necessary.

N.B. Make sure the number of cables is a multiple of four to get an even pattern on the front and back. The number of stitches for the pattern must be a multiple of eight. Cable pattern on 3.5mm (UK 10/US 4) needles over 8 stitches: k4, p1, k2, p1. Add enough extra stitches in the last row of the ribbing: increase approx. 1–2 per cable, based on your tension (gauge). For the sleeves, pick up the stitches around the armhole and add enough stitches to knit the pattern. For the sleeve cuff, decrease any extra stitches.

Measurements

WIDTH: 2 x 44cm (17½in) = 88cm (34¾in)

SHOULDERS: 13.5cm (5¼in)

NECK: 14cm (5½in)

NECKLINE DEPTH: 4–5cm (1½–2in)

ARMHOLE HEIGHT: 18cm (7in)

HEIGHT UP TO ARMHOLE, EXCL. RIBBING: 34cm (13½in)

SLEEVE LENGTH, EXCL. RIBBING: 34cm (13½in)

WRIST CIRCUMFERENCE: approx. 16cm (6¼in)

RIBBING: 4–6cm (1½–2¼in), as preferred

Materials

∞ 15 balls SMC Merino Extrafine 120 in 0150 Marine, or equivalent DK (light worsted/8-ply) yarn in dark blue; 50g/131yd/120m

∞ 3mm (UK 11/US 2) and 3.5mm (UK 10/US 4) circular needles

∞ 3.5mm (UK 10/US 4) straight needles

∞ cable needle

TENSION (GAUGE): 36 sts x 34 rows on 3.5mm (UK 10/US 4) needles in cable motif = 10 x 10cm (4 x 4in)

RIBBING: k1, p1

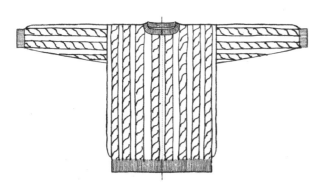

DETAIL FROM FIG. 75 ON PAGE 65

HAT

Choose a hat pattern and incorporate the cable pattern into it. Make sure the number of stitches is a multiple of eight.

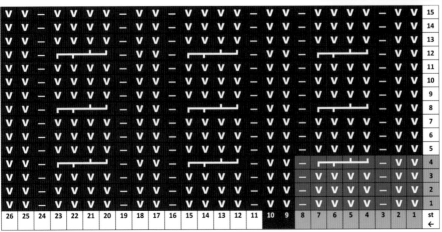

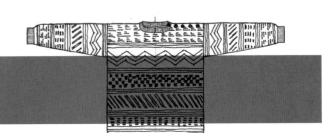

KATWIJK 7 GANSEY

AGE: 7–8 YEARS (SIZE: 128CM/4FT 2½IN),
CHEST CIRCUMFERENCE: 62CM (24½IN) + 4CM (1½IN) = 66CM (26IN), TOTAL HEIGHT: 47CM (18½IN)
Knit a swatch first, with different sized needles if necessary. A gansey should not be too loosely knitted. Follow the chart for the motif and adjust the width and/or height to your size, the yarn used and your tension (gauge). Follow the general instructions for knitting ganseys on page 51 and adjust where necessary.

Measurements

WIDTH: 2 x 33cm (13in) = 66cm (26in)

SHOULDERS: 10cm (4in)

NECK: 13cm (5¼in)

NECKLINE DEPTH: 3–4cm (1¼–1½in)

ARMHOLE HEIGHT: 15–16cm (6–6¼in)

HEIGHT UP TO ARMHOLE, EXCL. RIBBING: 30cm (11¾in)

SLEEVE LENGTH, EXCL. RIBBING: 32cm (12½in)

WRIST CIRCUMFERENCE: approx. 19cm (7½in)

RIBBING: 3–4cm (1¼–1½in), as preferred

Materials

∞ 8 balls of De Rerum Natura Ulysse 5-ply in Sel, or equivalent 5-ply (sport) yarn in cream; 50g/202yd/185m

∞ 2mm (UK 14/US 0) and 2.5mm (UK 13/US 1) circular needles

∞ 2.5mm (UK 13/US 1) straight needles

∞ 5 buttons

TENSION (GAUGE): 26 sts x 45 rows on 2.5mm (UK 13/US 1) needles = 10 x 10cm (4 x 4in)

RIBBING: k1, p1

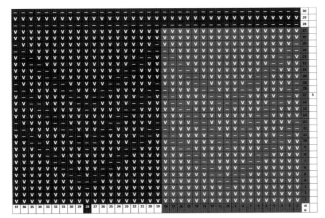

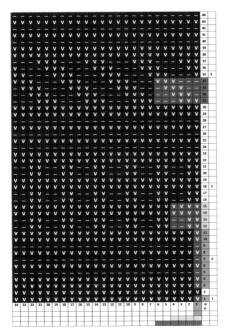

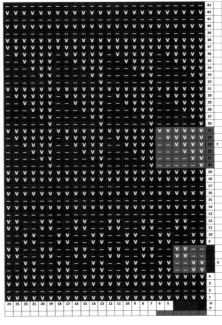

DETAIL FROM FIG. 72 ON PAGE 64

SOUTH HOLLAND
SCHEVENINGEN

Scheveningen's main source of income was fishing. Men, women and children worked at the fish auction, in fish processing, and in the fish trade. Baskets, nets, sails and barrels were also produced here for the fishing industry. Because the children had to work from an early age, it was almost impossible for them to get a proper education. In the town, there was a clear social difference between the ship owners and the fishermen. The fishermen (captains, mates and sailors) lived in the old village, north or south of the old shopping street, Keizerstraat, or in the houses in the Renbaan quarter which were built later. The ship owners, fish traders and other entrepreneurs lived in larger town houses, for example on the Stevinstraat.

A study of the living conditions in the old village (fig. 38, page 26) clearly shows that of the more than 3,000 houses surveyed, most were unfit for habitation – 1,727 houses had only one room. The others had two, at most three. Sometimes rooms were less than 6m² (19½ft²) . Many houses were smaller than 2.5m² (8ft²). More than a third had their own toilet, but it was not uncommon to have one toilet per seven houses (or about forty people). In 1866, four per cent of the population of Scheveningen died in a severe cholera epidemic.

Scheveningen ganseys are plain, with a patterned yoke surrounded with a decorative ridge. The main part of the gansey is knitted in stocking (stockinette) stitch.

77 CLASS AT THE PRINSES JULIANA SCHOOL AROUND 1900. MRS NOORDERVLIET-JOL, SCHEVENINGEN

78 *BOMSCHUIT* FROM SCHEVENINGEN IN A PORT IN SCOTLAND, AFTER THE LIFTING OF THE GUTTING BAN IN 1857, CA. 1900.

SCHEVENINGEN 6 GANSEY

AGE: 13–14 YEARS (SIZE: 164CM/5FT 4½IN), CHEST CIRCUMFERENCE: 84CM (33IN) + 4CM (1½IN) = 88CM (34¾IN), TOTAL HEIGHT: 56–58CM (22–22¾IN)

Knit a swatch first, with different sized needles if necessary. A gansey should not be too loosely knitted. Follow the chart for the motif and adjust the width and/or height to your size, the yarn used and your tension (gauge). In this case, the p2 next to the cables is changed to p1. Follow the general instructions for knitting ganseys on page 51 and adjust where necessary.

Measurements

WIDTH: 2 × 44CM (17½IN)= 88CM (34¾IN)

SHOULDERS: 13.5CM (5¼IN)

NECK: 14CM (5½IN)

NECKLINE DEPTH: 4–5CM (1½–2IN)

ARMHOLE HEIGHT: 18CM (7IN)

HEIGHT UP TO ARMHOLE, EXCL. RIBBING: 34CM (13½IN)

SLEEVE LENGTH, EXCL. RIBBING: 34CM (13½IN)

WRIST CIRCUMFERENCE: approx. 16CM (6¼IN)

RIBBING: 4–6CM (1½–2¼IN), as preferred

Materials

∞ 6 balls Scheepjes Zuiderzee in 2, or equivalent aran (worsted/10-ply) yarn in cornflower blue; 100g/218yd/199m

∞ 3.5mm (UK 10/US 4) and 4mm (UK 8/US 6) circular needles

∞ 4mm (UK 8/US 6) straight needles

∞ cable needle

TENSION (GAUGE): 20 sts x 28 rows on 4mm (UK 8/ US 6) needles = 10 x 10cm (4 x 4in)

RIBBING: k2, p2

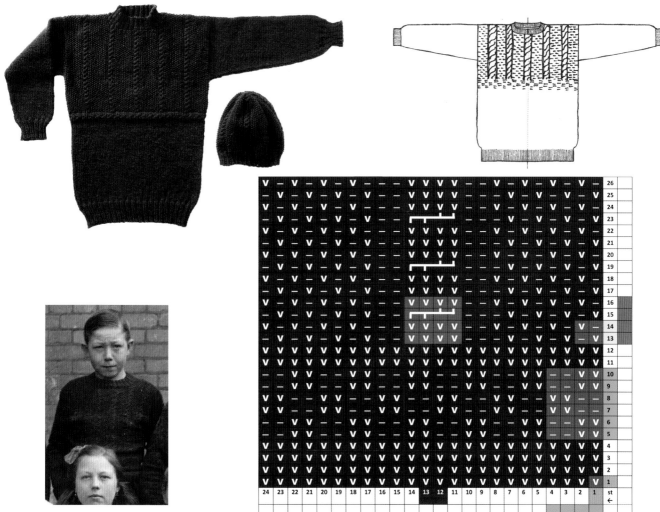

DETAIL FROM FIG. 78, OPPOSITE

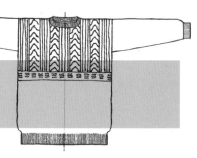

SCHEVENINGEN 7 GANSEY

AGE: 1½–2 YEARS (SIZE: 92CM/3FT ¼IN), CHEST CIRCUMFERENCE: 56CM (22IN) + 4CM (1½IN) = 60CM (23½IN), TOTAL HEIGHT: 36CM (14¼IN)

Knit a swatch first, with different sized needles if necessary. A gansey should not be too loosely knitted. Follow the chart for the motif and adjust the width and/or height to your size, the yarn used and your tension (gauge). Follow the general instructions for knitting ganseys on page 51 and adjust where necessary.

Measurements

WIDTH: 2 x 30cm (11¾in = 60cm (23½in)

SHOULDERS: 9cm (3½in)

NECK: 12cm (4¾in)

NECKLINE DEPTH: 3–4cm (1¼–1½in)

ARMHOLE HEIGHT: 13cm (5¼in)

HEIGHT UP TO ARMHOLE, EXCL. RIBBING: 22cm (8¾in)

SLEEVE LENGTH, EXCL. RIBBING: 23cm (9in)

WRIST CIRCUMFERENCE: approx. 12cm (4¾in)

RIBBING: 3–4cm (1¼–1½in), as preferred

Materials

∞ 4 balls Scheepjes Cotton 8 in 506, or equivalent 4-ply (fingering) yarn in jeans blue; 50g/186yd/170m

∞ 2mm (UK 14/US 0) and 2.5mm (UK 13/US 1) circular needles

∞ 2.5mm (UK 13/US 1) straight needles

∞ cable needle

TENSION (GAUGE): 28 sts x 40 rows on 2.5mm (UK 13/US 1) needles = 10 x 10cm (4 x 4in)

RIBBING: k2, p2

PERNIS

As early as 1830, fishermen left Pernis with longliners to catch fresh cod and haddock. The *Rotterdamsche Courant* of 22 May 1830 can testify to this: 'Rotterdam, May 21st. At the shipyard of D. Pons in Pernis, the fishing sloop named *De Eersteling van Pernis* was completed, built by shipwright Pieter Hoogland for account of D. Pons.' They sailed to the northernmost waters near Iceland and Greenland. Vlaardingen Museum has a pair of colourful two-thumb mittens in its collection, which most probably originate from

the Westfjords in the north-west of Iceland and possibly belonged to a fisherman from Pernis. Because these fishermen were the first to come into contact with their English and Scottish colleagues, they were probably also the first to adopt the wearing of ganseys as outerwear. This can still be seen in the design of the ganseys: the yoke resembles the smocked *keels* that were worn before.

In 1857, the Pernis longliner fleet consisted of seven sloops, five *bezanen* and seven *schokkers*.

79 *KOFFIEKOKER* OR *PRIKKENBIJTER* FROM PERNIS, CA. 1900. PERNIS HISTORICAL ASSOCIATION

80 YOUNG FISHERMEN FROM PERNIS, LEFT HUIG DE JONG, RIGHT HIS BROTHER ADRIANUS, 1902. PERNIS HISTORICAL ASSOCIATION

81 THE PORT OF PERNIS WITH LONGLINERS, AROUND 1910. PERNIS HISTORICAL ASSOCIATION

PERNIS 4 GANSEY

AGE: 13–14 YEARS (SIZE: 164CM/5FT 4¼IN), CHEST CIRCUMFERENCE: 84CM (33IN) + 4CM (1½IN) = 88CM (34¾IN), TOTAL HEIGHT: 56–58CM (22–22¾IN)

Knit a swatch first, with different sized needles if necessary. A gansey should not be too loosely knitted. Follow the chart for the motif and adjust the width and/or height to your size, the yarn used and your tension (gauge). In this case, the charts start and end with four rounds of stocking (stockinette) stitch instead of two rounds, to get sufficient height. Follow the general instructions for knitting ganseys on page 51 and adjust where necessary.

Measurements

WIDTH: 2 × 44CM = 88CM (34¾IN)

SHOULDERS: 13.5CM (5¼IN)

NECK: 14CM (5½IN)

NECKLINE DEPTH: 4–5CM (1½–2IN)

ARMHOLE HEIGHT: 18CM (7IN)

HEIGHT UP TO ARMHOLE, EXCL. RIBBING:
    34CM (13½IN)

SLEEVE LENGTH, EXCL. RIBBING: 34CM (13½IN)

WRIST CIRCUMFERENCE: approx. 16CM (6¼IN)

RIBBING: 4–6CM (1½–2¼IN), as preferred

Materials

∞ 10 balls Lang Thema Nuova in 0035, or equivalent 5-ply (sport) yarn in medium blue; 50g/129yd/118m

∞ 2.5mm (UK 13/US 1) and 3mm (UK 11/US 2) circular needles

∞ 3mm (UK 11/US 2) straight needle

TENSION (GAUGE): 25 sts × 31 rows on 3mm (UK 11/US 2) needles = 10 × 10cm (4 × 4in)

RIBBING: k2, p2

DETAIL FROM FIG. 79 ON PAGE 73

SHOULDER

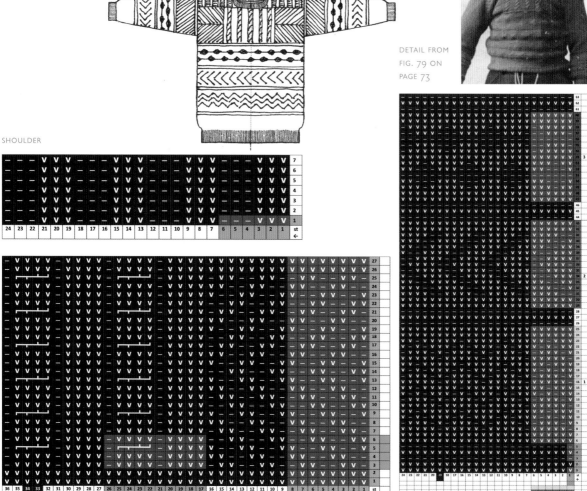

PERNIS 5 GANSEY

AGE: 12–13 YEARS (SIZE: 158CM/5FT 2¼IN), CHEST CIRCUMFERENCE: 80CM (31½IN) + 4CM (1½IN) = 84CM (33IN), TOTAL HEIGHT: 58CM (22¾IN)

Knit a swatch first, with different sized needles if necessary. A gansey should not be too loosely knitted. Follow the chart for the motif and adjust the width and/or height to your size, the yarn used and your tension (gauge). Follow the general instructions for knitting ganseys on page 51 and adjust where necessary.

Measurements

WIDTH: 2 × 42CM (16½IN) = 84CM (33IN)

SHOULDERS: 13.5CM (5¼IN)

NECK: 15CM (6IN)

NECKLINE DEPTH: 4–5CM (1½–2IN)

ARMHOLE HEIGHT: 18CM (7IN)

HEIGHT UP TO ARMHOLE, EXCL. RIBBING: 36CM (14¼IN)

SLEEVE LENGTH, EXCL. RIBBING: 38CM (15IN)

WRIST CIRCUMFERENCE: approx. 21CM (8¼IN)

RIBBING: 4–5CM (1½–2in), as preferred

Materials

∞ 6 balls Scheepjes Zuiderzee in 2, or equivalent aran (worsted/10-ply) yarn in cornflower blue; 100g/218yd/199m

∞ 3.5mm (UK 10/US 4) and 4.5mm (UK 7/US 7) circular needles

∞ 4.5mm (UK 7/US 7) straight needles

TENSION (GAUGE): 23 sts × 32 rows on 4.5mm (UK 7/US 7) needles in stocking (stockinette) stitch = 10 × 10cm (4 × 4in)

RIBBING: k2, p2

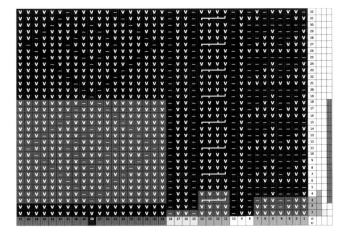

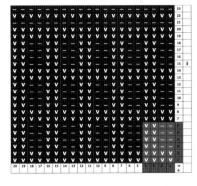

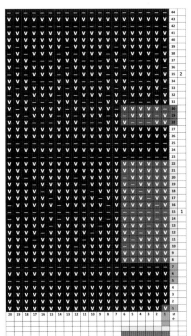

SOUTH HOLLAND
VLAARDINGEN

The large herring fleet of Vlaardingen was the linchpin on the Nieuwe Maas River and dominated the very lucrative herring fishery from the seventeenth century. The Vlaardingen fishing vessels – *haringbuizen* and *hoekers* – were allowed to gut herring on board, just like the Maassluis fleet, while the other fleets were strictly forbidden to bring gutted herring ashore. After the lifting of the gutting ban in 1857 and the introduction of the fast sailing lugger in 1866, the port of Vlaardingen filled up with fleets from Scheveningen and Katwijk, which also adopted the lugger. These towns did not have a port themselves and previously fished just off the coast, using flat-bottomed boats which sailed from the beach. Because the lugger had a keel, they had to move to a port, and the port of Vlaardingen was big enough. In Vlaardingen, a Scheveningen 'district' was created, where the women would knit ganseys with Scheveningen patterns and motifs. Fishermen from all over the country would flock to Vlaardingen to sign on. Longliners from Vlaardingen also sailed to the seas far north to catch cod and haddock. In winter, adapted herring luggers were deployed for this purpose. In addition, there was a lively supply industry of, among others, coopers, rope makers, shipyards and net knitters. Widows from Vlaardingen earned some extra money by knitting ganseys, which is why the patterns from Vlaardingen can be found on photographs from various fishing villages. They knew their own patterns by heart.

The Vlaardingen ganseys incorporated countless motifs, often built up from horizontal bands, sometimes with a yoke like the Pernis gansey but simpler. For more motifs, also see *Dutch Traditional Ganseys* and *More Traditional Dutch Ganseys*.

82 YOUNG FISHERMEN ON A BENCH AT THE PRIKKENGAT, AT THE CORNER OF THE PARALLELWEG/OLD PORT: CREW MEMBERS OF THE VL 171 *STELLA MATUTINA* PREPARING THE LONGLINES. TOP, FROM LEFT TO RIGHT: SMIT, ABR. VAN DORP, JOH. VERBOON. BOTTOM: A. VAN ROON, A. VAN DORP, J. BOERDAM. IN THE FOREGROUND, A *BENNE* (BASKET) WITH LONGLINE, CA. 1905

83 WOODEN SAILING LUGGER VL 19 CATO OWNED BY FISHING COMPANY J.H. WARNEKE, BETWEEN 1897 AND 1913. VLAARDINGEN CITY ARCHIVES

VLAARDINGEN 8 GANSEY

AGE: 1½–2 YEARS (SIZE: 92CM/3FT ¼IN), CHEST CIRCUMFERENCE: 56CM (22IN) + 4CM (1½IN) = 60CM (23½IN), TOTAL HEIGHT: 36CM (14¼IN)

Knit a swatch first, with different sized needles if necessary. A gansey should not be too loosely knitted. Follow the chart for the motif and adjust the width and/or height to your size, the yarn used and your tension (gauge). Follow the general instructions for knitting ganseys on page 51 and adjust where necessary.

Measurements

WIDTH: 2 x 30CM (11¾IN) = 60cm (23½in)

SHOULDERS: 9cm (3½in)

NECK: 12cm (4¾in)

NECKLINE DEPTH: 3–4cm (1¼–1½in)

ARMHOLE HEIGHT: 13cm (5¼in)

HEIGHT UP TO ARMHOLE, EXCL. RIBBING: 22cm (8¾in)

SLEEVE LENGTH, EXCL. RIBBING: 23cm (9in)

WRIST CIRCUMFERENCE: approx. 12cm (4¾in)

RIBBING: 3–4cm (1¼–1½in), as preferred

Materials

∞ 4 balls Rowan Wool Cotton 4-ply in 495 Marine, or equivalent 4-ply (fingering) yarn in dark blue; 50g/197yd/180m

∞ 2.5mm (UK 13/US 1) and 3mm (UK 11/US 2) circular needles

∞ 3mm (UK 11/US 2) straight needles

TENSION (GAUGE): 24 sts x approx. 38–42 rows on 3mm (UK 11/US 2) needles = 10 x 10cm (4 x 4in)

RIBBING: k1, p1

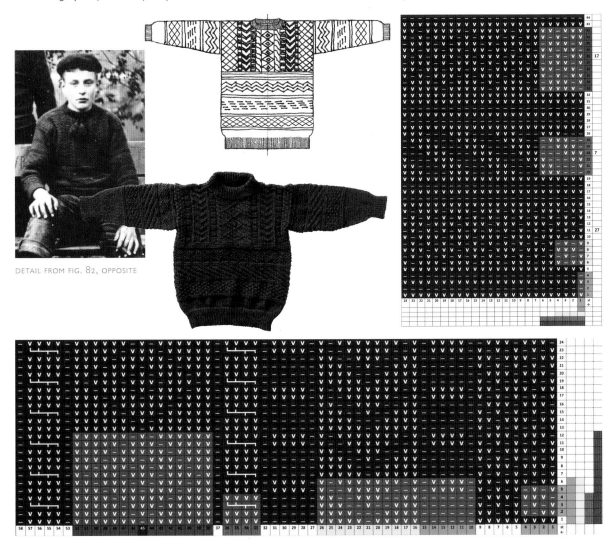

DETAIL FROM FIG. 82, OPPOSITE

VLAARDINGEN 9 GANSEY

AGE: 13–14 YEARS (SIZE: 164CM/5FT 4½IN), CHEST CIRCUMFERENCE: 84CM (33IN) + 4CM (1½IN) = 88CM (34¾IN), TOTAL HEIGHT: 56–58CM (22–22¾IN)

Knit a swatch first, with different sized needles if necessary. A gansey should not be too loosely knitted. Follow the chart for the motif and adjust the width and/or height to your size, the yarn used and your tension (gauge). The chart below applies to the bottom motif and the yoke. For the other motif charts refer to More Traditional Dutch Ganseys, *page 84, from bottom to top: motifs 3, 4 and 9. Follow the general instructions for knitting ganseys on page 51 and adjust where necessary.*

Measurements

WIDTH: 2 × 44CM (17½IN) = 88cm (34¾in)
SHOULDERS: 13.5CM (5¼IN)
NECKLINE DEPTH: 4–5CM (1½–2IN)
ARMHOLE HEIGHT: 18CM (7IN)
HEIGHT UP TO ARMHOLE, EXCL. RIBBING: 34CM (13½IN)
SLEEVE LENGTH, EXCL. RIBBING: 34CM (13½IN)
WRIST CIRCUMFERENCE: approx. 16CM (6¼IN)
RIBBING: 4–6CM (1½–2¼IN), as preferred

Materials

∞ 5 balls Scheepjes Zuiderzee in 3, or equivalent aran (worsted/10-ply) yarn in beige; 100g/218yd/199m
∞ 4mm (UK 8/US 6) and 4.5mm (UK 7/US 7) circular needles
∞ 4.5mm (UK 7/US 7) straight needles
TENSION (GAUGE): 19 sts × 24 rows on 4.5mm (UK 7/US 7) needles = 10 × 10cm (4 × 4in)
RIBBING: k1, p1

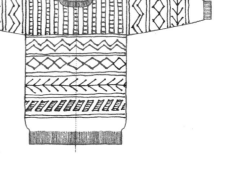

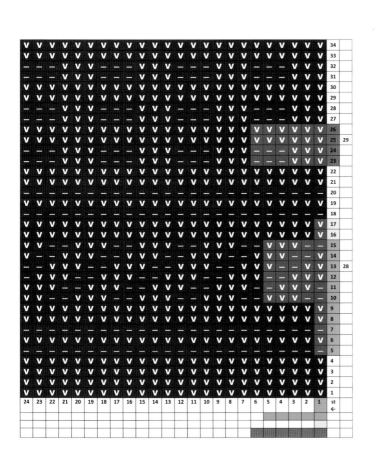

DETAIL OF ARIE VAN ROON IN A GANSEY WITH A YOKE, FROM FIG. 82 ON PAGE 76

SOUTH HOLLAND VOORNE-PUTTEN
ZWARTEWAAL

For Zwartewaal, water was the lifeblood of the community`. Sturgeon and salmon were already being fished on the river Meuse in Roman times. In the Middle Ages, shipping and fishing flourished. Fishermen from Zwartewaal mainly used longliners: they fished with lines and hooks to catch cod, and used live bait like lamprey (*prik* in Dutch).

Zwartewaal had a tidal port, meaning that the ships could only enter at high tide. When the Meuse estuary had fully silted up and was dammed up, the fleet disappeared; around 1900, ships were laid up or moved to the ports of Vlaardingen or IJmuiden.

The design of the ganseys, derived from the smock, is similar to that of Pernis. The ganseys are richly patterned and the fishermen here were probably the first to wear them as outerwear. In Zwartewaal, the ganseys were mainly knitted in Nassau blue: blue spun with a thin red fibre.

85 DETAIL, THE SPACER PROBABLY CAME FROM ZWARTEWAAL. ZWARTEWAAL 5 GANSEY

ZWARTEWAAL 5 GANSEY

AGE: 7–8 YEARS (SIZE: 128CM/4FT 2½IN), CHEST CIRCUMFERENCE: 62CM (24½IN) + 4CM (1½IN) = 66CM (26IN), TOTAL HEIGHT: 47CM (18½IN)

Knit a swatch first, with different sized needles if necessary. A gansey should not be knit too loosely. Follow the chart for the motif and adjust the width and/or height to your size, the yarn used and your tension (gauge). Follow the general instructions for knitting ganseys on page 51 and adjust where necessary.

Measurements

WIDTH: 2 x 33CM (13IN) = 66cm (26in)

SHOULDERS: 10cm (4in)

NECK: 13cm (5¼in)

NECKLINE DEPTH: 3–4cm (1¼–1½in)

ARMHOLE HEIGHT: 15–16cm (6–6¼in)

HEIGHT UP TO ARMHOLE, EXCL. RIBBING: 30cm (11¾in)

SLEEVE LENGTH, EXCL. RIBBING: 32cm (12½in)

WRIST CIRCUMFERENCE: approx. 19cm (7½in)

RIBBING: 3–4cm (1¼–1½in), as preferred

Materials

∞ 7 balls Scheepjes Merino Soft in 611 Mondrian, or equivalent DK (light worsted/8-ply) yarn in royal blue; 50g/115yd/105m

∞ 3mm (UK 11/US 2) and 3.5mm (UK 10/US 4) circular needles

∞ 3.5mm (UK 10/US 4) straight needles

TENSION (GAUGE): 22 sts x 34 rows on 3.5mm (UK 10/US 4) needles in stocking (stockinette) stitch = 10 x 10cm (4 x 4in); motifs 1 and 2: 23 sts x 36 rows = 10 x 10cm (4 x 4in); motif 3 (centre V-pattern): 23 sts x 40 rows = 10 x 10cm (4 x 4in)

RIBBING: k1, p1

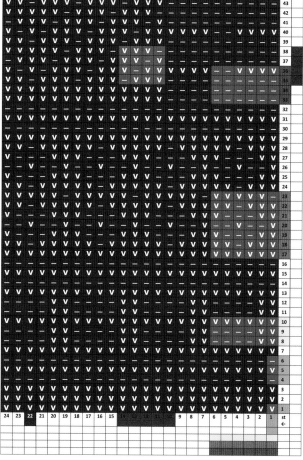

HAT

The hat uses the centre pattern of the gansey. Search the Internet for a suitable hat or beanie pattern. Here, I cast on 92 sts with 3mm (UK 11/US 2) needles, and started with k1, p1 ribbing. Then I switched to 3.5mm (UK 10/US 4) needles and knitted in stocking (stockinette) stitch without increasing, to make the ribbing fold outwards. Then I knitted four V-pattern panels, with 2 purl stitches in between.

The decreases were placed above the 2 purl stitches. In each second round, decrease on either side of the centre of these 2 stitches. Decrease until you have few stitches left, cut the yarn and pull through the remaining stitches.

In Middelharnis the most important form of sea fishing was longliner fishing with sloops. A summer longliner for cod fishing comprised about 3,600 hook sets, while the winter longliner for haddock fishing could have up to 7,000. Due to silting up of the port and a few years with very poor catches, the fishermen lived under abominable conditions and many of them moved to Vlaardingen and IJmuiden, where there was more work. The ship owners eventually also moved their longliners to IJmuiden.

The Middelharnis ganseys are characterized by a front placket.

86 KEES AND ADRIANUS VAN DER SLUIS, CA. 1900.
GOEREE-OVERFLAKKEE REGIONAL ARCHIVE
87 THE PORT OF MIDDELHARNIS WITH LONGLINERS,
CA. 1900

MIDDELHARNIS 5 GANSEY

AGE: 13–14 YEARS (SIZE: 164CM/5FT 4½IN), CHEST CIRCUMFERENCE: 84CM (33IN) + 4CM (1½IN) = 88CM (34¾IN), TOTAL HEIGHT: 56–58CM (22–22¾IN)

Knit a swatch first, with different sized needles if necessary. A gansey should not be too loosely knitted. Follow the chart for the motif and adjust the width and/or height to your size, the yarn used and your tension (gauge). Follow the general instructions for knitting ganseys on page 51 and adjust where necessary.

Measurements

WIDTH: 2 × 44IN (17½IN)= 88cm (34¾in)

SHOULDERS: 13.5cm (5¼in)

NECK: 14cm (5½in)

NECKLINE DEPTH: 4–5cm (1½–2in)

ARMHOLE HEIGHT: 18cm (7in)

HEIGHT UP TO ARMHOLE, EXCL. RIBBING: 34cm (13½in)

SLEEVE LENGTH, EXCL. RIBBING: 34cm (13½in)

WRIST CIRCUMFERENCE: approx. 16cm (6¼in)

RIBBING: 4–6cm (1½–2¼in), as preferred

Materials

∞ 12 balls Lang Thema Nuova in 0035, or equivalent 5-ply (sport) yarn in medium blue; 50g/129yd/118m

∞ 2.5mm (UK 13/US 1) and 3mm (UK 11/US 2) circular needles

∞ 3mm (UK 11/US 2) straight needles

∞ 4 buttons

TENSION (GAUGE): 30 sts × 42 rows on 3mm (UK 11/US 2) needles = 10 x 10cm (4 x 4in)

RIBBING: k1, p1

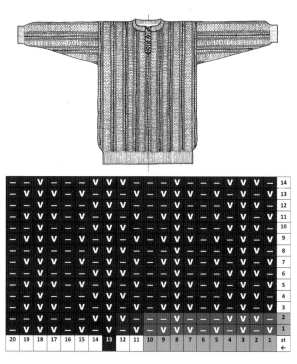

VARIATION

83

ZEELAND NOORD-BEVELAND
COLIJNSPLAAT

Colijnsplaat was founded in 1598 after the reclamation of more land. The foundations of the village were determined by setting the perimeter as a rectangle and digging straight trenches for the plots. This rectangular pattern has been preserved. Because of the port, dug in 1599, Colijnsplaat was an attractive trade hub. Two plague epidemics, close together, in the seventeenth century proved disastrous for the population, and caused trade and the port to come to a standstill. It wasn't until the second half of the seventeenth century that living conditions improved. Many fishermen from Veer Vlissingen and Arnemuiden settled in Colijnsplaat after 1961 when the Veerse Gat dam was completed, because their villages had been cut off from the open sea.

88 IN THE PORT OF COLIJNSPLAAT, CA. 1950.
MARITIME MUSEUM ROTTERDAM

89 PORT OF COLIJNSPLAAT AROUND 1900

COLIJNSPLAAT GANSEY

AGE: 10–11 YEARS (SIZE: 146CM/4FT 9½IN), CHEST CIRCUMFERENCE: 71CM (28IN) + 3CM (1¼IN) = 74CM (29¼IN), TOTAL HEIGHT: 56CM (22IN)

Knit a swatch first, with different sized needles if necessary. A gansey should not be too loosely knitted. Follow the chart for the motif and adjust the width and/or height to your size, the yarn used and your tension (gauge). Follow the general instructions for knitting ganseys on page 51 and adjust where necessary.

Measurements

WIDTH: 2 x 37CM (14½IN = 74cm (29¼in)
SHOULDERS: 11.5cm (4½in)
NECK: 14cm (5½in)
NECKLINE DEPTH: 3–4cm (1¼–1½in)
ARMHOLE HEIGHT: 17cm (6¾in)
HEIGHT UP TO ARMHOLE, EXCL. RIBBING: 33cm (13in)
SLEEVE LENGTH, EXCL. RIBBING: 38cm (15in)
WRIST CIRCUMFERENCE: approx. 20cm (8in)
RIBBING: 4–5cm (1½–2in), as preferred

Materials

∞ 8 balls SMC Merino Extrafine 120 in 0154 Jeans, or equivalent DK (light worsted/8-ply) yarn in jeans blue; 50g/131yd/120m
∞ 3.5mm (UK 10/US 4) and 4mm (UK 8/US 6) circular needles
∞ 4mm (UK 8/US 6) straight needles

TENSION (GAUGE): 22 sts x 30 rows on 4mm (UK 8/US 6) needles = 10 x 10cm (4 x 4in)

RIBBING: k1, p1

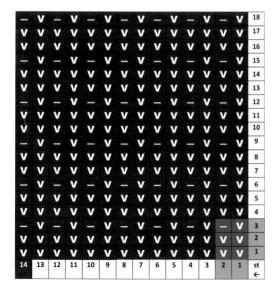

ZEELAND ZUID-BEVELAND
YERSEKE

In the ninth century, the German emperor Otto II granted the monks of Bavel and the monastery of Nivelles the right to mine peat on the island of Zuid-Beveland. It is not known what the region was called in those days. Some assume that the name comes from Roman times: they called the area 'Trembling Land' (*Bevend Land*), because it would tremble under your feet even on higher sand ridges.

Yerseke was founded as a stopping place, and agriculture was the main activity. After the Felix flood in 1530, Yerseke got access to open water, which was handy for shipping agricultural goods. Only in the mid-nineteenth century did the population switch to the cultivation of oysters and mussels, something the town is famous for today. Unfortunately, this is now being threatened by exotic winkles that drill holes in the shells and kill the molluscs.

Around 1900, everyone, young and old, men, women and children, worked in the oyster pits, for very little money.

A number of different ganseys have been found in Yerseke.

90 CLEANING THE PANS, 1911. ZEELAND LIBRARY
91 OYSTER FISHERMEN FROM YERSEKE, CA. 1920. ZEELAND LIBRARY

YERSEKE 2 GANSEY

AGE: 7–8 YEARS (SIZE: 128CM/4FT 2½IN), CHEST CIRCUMFERENCE: 62CM (24½IN) + 4CM (1½IN) = 66CM (26IN), TOTAL HEIGHT: 47CM (18½IN)

Knit a swatch first, with different sized needles if necessary. A gansey should not be too loosely knitted. Follow the chart for the motif and adjust the width and/or height to your size, the yarn used and your tension (gauge). Follow the general instructions for knitting ganseys on page 51 and adjust where necessary.

Measurements

WIDTH: 2 × 33cm (13in) = 66cm (26in)

SHOULDERS: 10cm (4in)

NECK: 13cm (5¼in)

NECKLINE DEPTH: 3–4cm (1¼–1½in)

ARMHOLE HEIGHT: 15–16cm (6–6¼in)

HEIGHT UP TO ARMHOLE, EXCL. RIBBING: 30cm (11¾in)

SLEEVE LENGTH, EXCL. RIBBING: 32cm (12½in)

WRIST CIRCUMFERENCE: approx. 19cm (7½in)

RIBBING: 3–4cm (1¼–1½in), as preferred

Materials

∞ 5 balls Scheepjes Cotton 8 in 527, or equivalent 4-ply (fingering) yarn in navy; 50g/186yd/170m

∞ 2mm (UK 14/US 0) and 2.5mm (UK 13/US 1) circular needles

∞ 2.5mm (UK 13/US 1) straight needles

TENSION (GAUGE): 33 sts × 44 rows on 2.5mm (UK 13/US 1) needles = 10 × 10cm (4 × 4in)

RIBBING: k1, p1

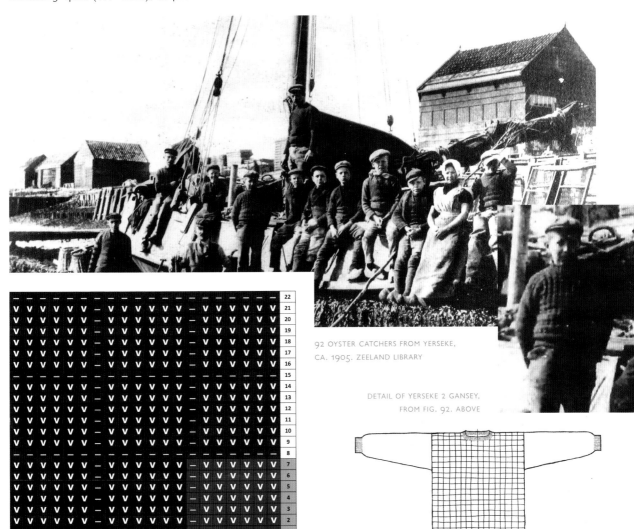

92 OYSTER CATCHERS FROM YERSEKE, CA. 1905. ZEELAND LIBRARY

DETAIL OF YERSEKE 2 GANSEY, FROM FIG. 92. ABOVE

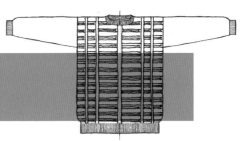

YERSEKE 5 GANSEY

AGE: 13–14 YEARS (SIZE: 164CM/5FT 4½IN), CHEST CIRCUMFERENCE: 84CM (33IN) + 4CM (1½IN) = 88CM (34¾IN), TOTAL HEIGHT: 56–58CM (22–22¾IN)

Knit a swatch first, with different sized needles if necessary. A gansey should not be too loosely knitted. Follow the chart for the motif and adjust the width and/or height to your size, the yarn used and your tension (gauge). Follow the general instructions for knitting ganseys on page 51 and adjust where necessary.

Measurements

WIDTH: 2 x 44cm (17½in) = 88cm (34¾in)

SHOULDERS: 13.5cm (5¼in)

NECK: 14cm (5½in)

NECKLINE DEPTH: 4–5cm (1½–2in)

ARMHOLE HEIGHT: 18cm (7in)

HEIGHT UP TO ARMHOLE, EXCL. RIBBING: 34cm (13½in)

SLEEVE LENGTH, EXCL. RIBBING: 34cm (13½in)

WRIST CIRCUMFERENCE: approx. 16cm (6¼in)

RIBBING: 4–6cm (1½–2¼in), as preferred

Materials

∞ 5 balls Scheepjes Zuiderzee in 2, or equivalent aran (worsted/10-ply) yarn in cornflower blue; 100g/218yd/199m

∞ 2.5mm (UK 13/US 1) and 3mm (UK 11/US 2) circular needles

∞ 3mm (UK 11/US 2) straight needles

TENSION (GAUGE): 20 sts x 28 rows on 3mm (UK 11/US 2) needles = 10 x 10cm (4 x 4in)

RIBBING: k2, p2

93 WORKING ON THE PANS WITH OYSTER BROOD, CA. 1905. ZEELAND LIBRARY
93A DETAIL OF YERSEKE 5 GANSEY

Oud-Arnemuiden was mentioned in historical documents as early as 1223. It was lost to the sea in 1440, was rebuilt, and was then swallowed up again twenty years later. Around 1462, Arnemuiden as we know it now was built. The port was of great importance to the province of Zeeland in the fifteenth and sixteenth centuries. There were often large numbers of merchant vessels anchored off the shore. In 1496, 135 ships arrived as escort of the Spanish princess Joanna (the later Joanna the Mad), who was on her way to Lier to marry Philip the Fair. In 1522, 150 ships sailed from Arnemuiden to collect Emperor Charles V from England.

In the seventeenth century, the port silted up and was no longer accessible for larger vessels. This brought merchant shipping to a standstill. The trade in salt did continue, but on a smaller scale. Many inhabitants left, and the salt trade further declined. The population started looking for different ways to make a living, and fishing became more important. In 1901, the Arnemuiden fleet consisted of sixty-five vessels. Although only a small percentage of the population still works in the industry, and the fleet is moored in nearby Vlissingen, Arnemuiden is still very much known as a fishing village.

The two most important motifs for the Arnemuiden gansey are the snake and the box.

94 HOOGAARZEN FROM ARNEMUIDEN IN THE PORT OF VEERE, JAN WILLEMSEN

ARNEMUIDEN 1 GANSEY

AGE: 11–12 YEARS (SIZE: 152CM/4FT 11¾IN), CHEST CIRCUMFERENCE: 76CM (30IN) + 4CM (1½IN) = 80CM (31½IN), TOTAL HEIGHT: APPROX. 55CM (21¾IN)

Knit a swatch first, with different sized needles if necessary. A gansey should not be too loosely knitted. Follow the chart for the motif and adjust the width and/or height to your size, the yarn used and your tension (gauge). Follow the general instructions for knitting ganseys on page 51 and adjust where necessary.

Measurements

WIDTH: 2 x 40cm (15¾in) = 80cm (31½in)

SHOULDERS: 13cm (5¼in)

NECK: 14cm (5½in)

NECKLINE DEPTH: 3–4cm (1¼–1½in)

ARMHOLE HEIGHT: 17cm (6¾in)

HEIGHT UP TO ARMHOLE, EXCL. RIBBING: 34cm (13½in)

SLEEVE LENGTH, EXCL. RIBBING: 36cm (14¼in)

WRIST CIRCUMFERENCE: approx. 20cm (8in)

RIBBING: 3–5cm (1¼-2in), as preferred

Materials

∞ 7 balls Rowan Pure Wool 4-ply in 410 Indigo, or equivalent 4-ply (fingering) yarn in indigo; 50g/174yd/159m

∞ 2.5mm (UK 13/US 1) circular needles

∞ 2.5mm (UK 13/US 1) straight needles

TENSION (GAUGE): 20 sts x 28 rows on 2.5mm (UK 13/US 1) needles = 10 x 10cm (4 x 4in)

RIBBING: k2, p2

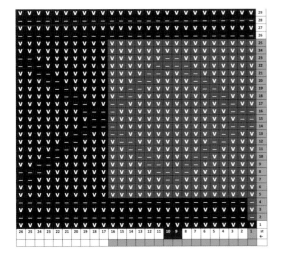

DETAIL OF BOY IN ARNEMUIDEN 1 GANSEY WITH SNAKE MOTIF, FROM FIG. 95, LEFT

95 FISHERMEN FROM ARNEMUIDEN IN THE PORT OF VLISSINGEN, CA. 1900. VLISSINGEN CITY ARCHIVES

ARNEMUIDEN 2 GANSEY

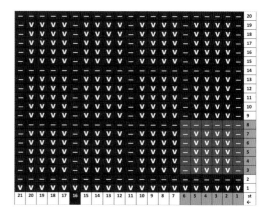

AGE: 10—11 YEARS (SIZE: 146CM/4FT 9IN), CHEST CIRCUMFERENCE: 71CM (28IN) + 3CM (1¼IN) = 74CM (29¼IN), TOTAL HEIGHT: 56CM (22IN)

Knit a swatch first, with different sized needles if necessary. A gansey should not be too loosely knitted. Follow the chart for the motif and adjust the width and/or height to your size, the yarn used and your tension (gauge). Follow the general instructions for knitting ganseys on page 51 and adjust where necessary.

Measurements

WIDTH: 2 x 37cm (14½in) = 74cm (29¼in)

SHOULDERS: 11.5cm (4½in)

NECK: 14cm (5½in)

NECKLINE DEPTH: 3—4cm (1¼-1½in)

ARMHOLE HEIGHT: 17cm (6¾in)

HEIGHT UP TO ARMHOLE, EXCL. RIBBING: 33cm (13in)

SLEEVE LENGTH, EXCL. RIBBING: 38cm (15in)

WRIST CIRCUMFERENCE: approx. 20cm (8in)

RIBBING: 4—5cm (1½—2in), as preferred

Materials

∞ 7—8 balls SMC Merino Extrafine 120 in 0156 Denim Blue, or equivalent DK (light worsted/8-ply) yarn in jeans blue; 50g/131yd/120m

∞ 3mm (UK 11/US 2) and 3.5mm (UK 10/US 4) circular needles

∞ 3.5mm (UK 10/US 4) straight needles

TENSION (GAUGE): 22 sts x 30 rows on 3.5mm (UK 10/US 4) needles = 10 x 10cm (4 x 4in)

RIBBING: k1, p1

DETAIL OF BOY WITH ARNEMUIDEN 2 GANSEY WITH BOX MOTIF, FROM FIG. 29 ON PAGE 19

ARNEMUIDEN 5 GANSEY

AGE: 11—12 YEARS (SIZE: 152CM/4FT 11¾IN), CHEST CIRCUMFERENCE: 76CM (30IN) + 4CM (1½IN) = 80CM (31½IN), TOTAL HEIGHT: APPROX. 55CM (21¾IN)

Knit a swatch first, with different sized needles if necessary. A gansey should not be too loosely knitted. Follow the chart for the motif and adjust the width and/or height to your size, the yarn used and your tension (gauge). Follow the general instructions for knitting ganseys on page 51 and adjust where necessary.

Measurements

WIDTH: 2 x 40cm (15¾in) = 80cm (31½in)

SHOULDERS: 13cm (5¼in)

NECK: 14cm (5½in)

NECKLINE DEPTH: 3—4cm (1¼—1½in)

ARMHOLE HEIGHT: 17cm (6¾in)

HEIGHT UP TO ARMHOLE, EXCL. RIBBING:
approx. 34cm (13½in)

SLEEVE LENGTH, EXCL. RIBBING: 36cm (14¼in)

WRIST CIRCUMFERENCE: approx. 20cm (8in)

RIBBING: 3—5cm (1¼—2in), as preferred

Materials

∞ 12 balls Scheepjes Super Noorsewol Extra in 1724, or equivalent DK (light worsted/8-ply) yarn in delft blue; 50g/87yd/80m

∞ 4mm (UK 8/US 6) and 4.5mm (UK 7/US 7) circular needles

∞ 4.5mm (UK 7/US 7) straight needles

∞ cable needle

TENSION (GAUGE): 20 sts x 28 rows on 4.5mm (UK 7/US 7) needles = 10 x 10cm (4 x 4in)

RIBBING: k2, p2

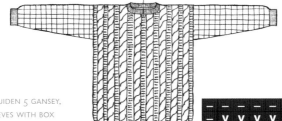

DETAIL OF BOY WITH ARNEMUIDEN 5 GANSEY, BODY WITH CABLES AND SLEEVES WITH BOX MOTIF (COMBINATION OF ARNEMUIDEN 4 AND 2 GANSEYS). FROM FIG. 29 ON PAGE 19

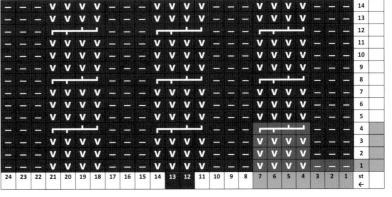

ZEELAND ZEEUWS-VLAANDEREN
DE PAAL

De Paal, a hamlet on the Westerschelde in the municipality of Grauw, close to the Drowned Land of Saeftinghe in Zeeuws-Vlaanderen at the Belgian border, was a small fishing village, where people mainly fished for mussels and shrimp. The mussels, cultivated in mussel banks, were sold in Antwerp. The fleet sailed under the code GRA, as De Paal was part of the larger fishing village of Graauw (now called Grauw). At De Paal, there was a shipyard, where *hengsten*, *lemmerhengsten* and *hoogaarzen* were built. The *hengst* was a vessel that was only built in Zeeuws-Vlaanderen. The name probably comes from the village of Hengstdijk. In the rest of Zeeland, it was seen as

improper to use a *hengst* for sailing, they preferred the *hoogaars*. An important activity here was mudding or *modderen*: at low tide, a mud tray would be filled up with a shovel, and then sailed out of the port when the tide came in. This was a way to ensure sufficient depth to berth boats on the quay. The small port of De Paal is now a marina.

96 *HENGST FROM DE PAAL*
97 FONS THEENAART GOES FISHING WITH HIS FATHER AS A YOUNG BOY

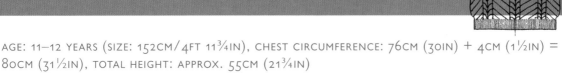

DE PAAL GANSEY

AGE: 11–12 YEARS (SIZE: 152CM/4FT 11¾IN), CHEST CIRCUMFERENCE: 76CM (30IN) + 4CM (1½IN) = 80CM (31½IN), TOTAL HEIGHT: APPROX. 55CM (21¾IN)

Knit a swatch first, with different sized needles if necessary. A gansey should not be too loosely knitted. Follow the chart for the motif and adjust the width and/or height to your size, the yarn used and your tension (gauge). Follow the general instructions for knitting ganseys on page 51 and adjust where necessary.

Measurements

WIDTH: 2 × 40cm (15¾in) = 80cm (31½in)

SHOULDERS: 13cm (5¼in)

NECK: 14cm (5½in)

NECKLINE DEPTH: 3–4cm (1¼–1½in)

ARMHOLE HEIGHT: 17cm (6¾in)

HEIGHT UP TO ARMHOLE, EXCL. RIBBING: 34cm (13½in)

SLEEVE LENGTH, EXCL. RIBBING: 36cm (14¼in)

WRIST CIRCUMFERENCE: approx. 20cm (8in)

RIBBING: 3–5cm (1¼–2in), as preferred

Materials

∞ 8 balls SMC Universa in 151 Indigo, or equivalent DK (light worsted/8-ply) yarn in indigo; 50g/136yd/125m

∞ 3mm (UK 11/US 2) and 3.5mm (UK 10/US 4) circular needles

∞ 3.5mm (UK 10/US 4) straight needles

∞ cable needle

TENSION (GAUGE): 20 sts × 28 rows on 3.5mm (UK 10/US 4) needles = 10 × 10cm (4 × 4in)

RIBBING: k2, p2

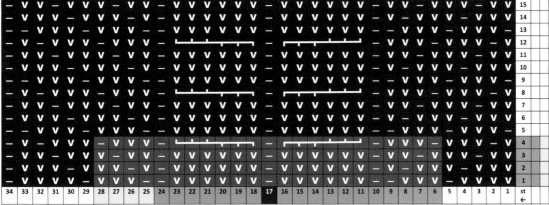

7 MAJOR RIVERS

There were many towns along the large rivers and inland waterways in the Netherlands where fishing was an important activity – Ammerstol, Gorinchem, Werkendam, Woudrichem, Willemstad, Drongelen, Heusden, Well, Bokhoven, Empel, Kerkdriel, Rossum, Heerewaarden, Lith, Lithoyen, Oyen, Brakel, Haaften, Harwenen, Hesselt, Ophemert, Lent, Ooij, Lesemond, Roon, Culemborg, Moerdijk, Hardinxveld, Charlois, Schiedam, Zwartsluis, Numansdorp, Dreumel, Vianen, Hellevoetsluis, Wilsum, Ohé en Laak and Westervoort en Arkel.

As national waterways, the rivers were usually leased out to fish traders. The river fishermen who caught salmon, sturgeon, herring, shad, white fish and eel, were at the mercy of the leaseholders, who squeezed the fishermen whenever they could,

threatening them with taking away their fishing licence. Sometimes, in bad weather, mainly in the winter, the traders would hand out advances for next year's catch, meaning the fisherman had their hands completely tied. To make it even worse, there were a lot of poachers who would rob the nets the fishermen put out. The poachers were not just other fishermen, but also miners from Limburg and Belgium, who were known to go on fishing raids along the river Meuse. This mostly happened on Sundays, when the fishermen had their day of rest.

Because of severe pollution of the rivers and inland waterways, and the construction of obstacles such as locks and dams, this type of fishing disappeared in the mid-twentieth century.

SOUTH HOLLAND
CHARLOIS

Charlois (pronounced 'Sharlows') was annexed by the municipality of Rotterdam in 1895. It is located in the De Reijerwaard area, gifted by Philip the Good to his son Charles the Bold in 1458. The latter determined that the diked area should 'from now on be referred to as the Land of Charollais'. It may be that he simply liked this name, which resembled his own. The county of Charolais in France, which also belonged to Charles the Bold, bore a similar name.

Charlois expanded in 1873, when Katendrecht was added and Rotterdam built a large port there. There was only a little bit of fishing happening at the time, mainly river fishing. The shipyards, however, were of great economic importance.

99 STAFF AT THE SHIPYARD, CA. 1930. HISTORICAL SOCIETY OF CHARLOIS

DETAIL OF A BOY IN A GANSEY
FROM FIG. 99, RIGHT

100 BOATS OWNED BY CAPTAIN BLOM. HISTORICAL SOCIETY OF CHARLOIS

CHARLOIS GANSEY

AGE: 13–14 YEARS (SIZE: 164CM/5FT 4½IN), CHEST CIRCUMFERENCE: 84CM (33IN) + 4CM (1½IN) = 88CM (34¾IN), TOTAL HEIGHT: 56–58CM (22–22¾IN)

Knit a swatch first, with different sized needles if necessary. A gansey should not be too loosely knitted. Follow the chart for the motif and adjust the width and/or height to your size, the yarn used and your tension (gauge). Follow the general instructions for knitting ganseys on page 51 and adjust where necessary.

Measurements

WIDTH: 2 × 44cm (17½in) = 88cm (34¾in)

SHOULDERS: 13.5cm (5¼in)

NECK: 14cm (5½in)

NECKLINE DEPTH: 4–5cm (1½–2in)

ARMHOLE HEIGHT: 18cm (7in)

HEIGHT UP TO ARMHOLE, EXCL. RIBBING: 34cm (13½in)

SLEEVE LENGTH, EXCL. RIBBING: 34cm (13½in)

WRIST CIRCUMFERENCE: approx. 16cm (6¼in)

RIBBING: 4–6cm (1½–2¼in), as preferred

Materials

∞ 12 balls Hjertegarn Vital in 6500, or equivalent DK (light worsted/8-ply) yarn in dark blue; 50g/126yd/115m

∞ 2.5mm (UK 13/US 1) and 3mm (UK 11/US 2) circular needles

∞ 3mm (UK 11/US 2) straight needles

TENSION (GAUGE): 23 sts × 34 rows in pattern on 3mm (UK 11/US 2) needles = 10 × 10cm (4 × 4in)

RIBBING: k2, p2

SCARF

Approx. 3 balls Hjertegarn Vital, 6500. On 3.5mm (UK 10/US 4) needles, cast on 38 sts. Knit 3 rows. Continue in pattern, starting with k2. When the work measures approx. 120cm (47in), knit 4 rows and cast off.

HAT

Approx. 1 ball Hjertegarn Vital, 6500. On 3mm (UK 11/US 2) needles, cast on 120 sts and close to knit in the round. Knit 3cm (1¼in) of k1, p1 ribbing. Switch to 3.5mm (UK 10/US 4) needles and continue with the pattern. Round 1: knit. Start the pattern with k4. Start decreasing when the work measures 15cm (6in), after a knit round: *k4, p2tog* to end (100 sts). Continue the pattern (work sts as before above each other) and on the fourth round, *k1, p2tog, k1, p1 * to end (80 sts). In the next fourth round, *slip 2 sts (as if to knit together), k1 and pass the 2 slipped sts over (the middle st is on top), p1* to end (40 sts). In the sixth round, k2tog to end. Cut the yarn and pull a double strand through the remaining 20 sts. Weave in the ends.

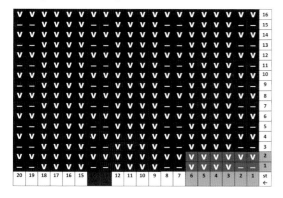

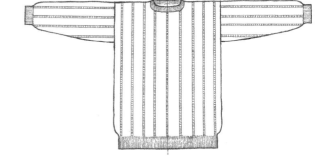

BRABANT
WOUDRICHEM

At Woudrichem, called Woerkum by the locals, the rivers Meuse and Waal come together and then form the Merwede. This fishing village has a remarkable history. Count Diederic Loeff van Horne, Lord of Altena, granted it city rights in 1356, and in 1362 the residents and their children were granted extensive fishing rights. After that Woudrichem had a lot of river fishermen, who were often very poor. Around 1900, the river fishing industry experienced an economic upturn. The fishermen, predominantly using salmon barges, caught a lot of salmon, which they were able to sell at the local auction for a good price. Sometimes, they would catch sturgeon. Later, they also fished using *galgen* and *schokkers*. These vessels can still be seen at the local fishing museum, in the Arsenaal in the Kerkstraat and in the old port.

To date, four different ganseys were found in Woudrichem, with variations on cables, lightning, ladders and squares.

101 SALMON FISHERMEN IN WOUDRICHEM, 1913.
ZUIDERZEE CRAFT FOUNDATION, ENKHUIZEN

'In the old days, the waters used to be teeming with salmon, eel and sturgeon. Salmon, in particular, was of economic importance. Around 1900, there were at least 300,000, perhaps half a million in our waters. Now they're gone. For several years now, large numbers of salmon and sturgeon have been released upstream in the major rivers. The question is whether the fish will ever return here. Even if it's only a thousand or so. Of course, this number is of no use for economic fishing, but it does benefit the diversity of the species.' Joop van Straaten

WOUDRICHEM 3 GANSEY

AGE: 7–8 YEARS (SIZE: 128CM/4FT 2½IN), CHEST CIRCUMFERENCE: 62CM (24½IN) + 4CM (1½IN) = 66CM (26IN), TOTAL HEIGHT: 47CM (18½IN)

Knit a swatch first, with different sized needles if necessary. A gansey should not be too loosely knitted. Follow the chart for the motif and adjust the width and/or height to your size, the yarn used and your tension (gauge). Follow the general instructions for knitting ganseys on page 51 and adjust where necessary.

Measurements

WIDTH: 2 × 33CM (13IN) = 66CM (26IN)

SHOULDERS: 10CM (4IN)

NECK: 13CM (5¼IN)

NECKLINE DEPTH: 3–4CM (1¼–1½IN)

ARMHOLE HEIGHT: 15–16CM (6–6¼IN)

HEIGHT UP TO ARMHOLE, EXCL. RIBBING:
    30CM (11¾IN)

SLEEVE LENGTH, EXCL. RIBBING: 32CM (12½IN)

WRIST CIRCUMFERENCE: approx. 19CM (7½IN)

RIBBING: 3–4CM (1¼–1½IN), as preferred

Materials

∞ 7 balls SMC Merino Extrafine 120 in 0155 Navy, or equivalent DK (light worsted/8-ply) yarn in navy; 50g/131yd/120m

∞ 3mm (UK 11/US 2) and 3.5mm (UK 10/US 4) circular needles

∞ 3.5mm (UK 10/US 4) straight needles

∞ cable needle

TENSION (GAUGE): 22 sts × 30 rows on 3.5mm (UK 10/ US 4) needles = 10 × 10cm (4 × 4in)

RIBBING: k2, p2

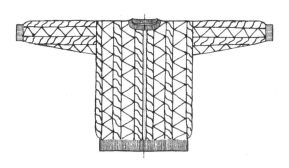

DETAIL OF BOY WEARING WOUDRICHEM 3 GANSEY, FROM FIG. 101 OPPOSITE

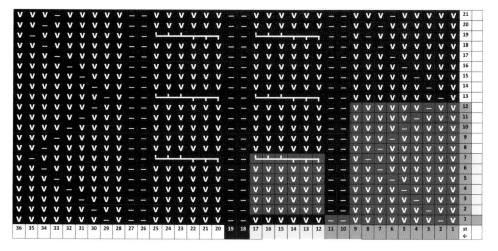

WOUDRICHEM 4 GANSEY

AGE: 11–12 YEARS (SIZE: 152CM/4FT 11¾IN), CHEST CIRCUMFERENCE: 76CM (30IN) +
4CM (1½IN) = 80CM (31½IN), TOTAL HEIGHT: APPROX. 55CM (21¾IN)

Knit a swatch first, with different sized needles if necessary. A gansey should not be too loosely knitted. Follow the chart for the motif and adjust the width and/or height to your size, the yarn used and your tension (gauge). Follow the general instructions for knitting ganseys on page 51 and adjust where necessary.

Measurements

WIDTH: 2 x 40cm (15¾in) = 80cm (31½in)

SHOULDERS: 13cm (5¼in)

NECK: 14cm (5½in)

NECKLINE DEPTH: 3–4cm (1¼–1½in)

ARMHOLE HEIGHT: 17cm (6¾in)

HEIGHT UP TO ARMHOLE EXCL. RIBBING:
    approx. 34cm (13½in)

SLEEVE LENGTH, EXCL. RIBBING: 36cm (14¼in)

WRIST CIRCUMFERENCE: approx. 20cm (8in)

RIBBING: 3–5cm (1¼–2in), as preferred

Materials

∞ 10 balls Hjertegarn Mini Vital in 698 Navy
    Blue, or equivalent 5-ply (sport) yarn in navy;
    50g/164yd/150m

∞ 2.5mm (UK 13/US 1) circular needles

∞ 2.5mm (UK 13/US 1) straight needles

∞ cable needle

TENSION (GAUGE): 36 sts x 40 rows on 2.5mm
(UK 13/US 1) needles = 10 x 10cm (4 x 4in)

RIBBING: k2, p2

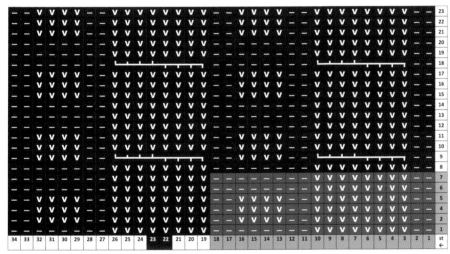

DETAIL OF WOUDRICHEM 4
GANSEY FROM FIG. 102, LEFT

102 SALMON FISHING IN WOUDRICHEM, CA. 1910.
ZUIDERZEE CRAFT FOUNDATION, ENKHUIZEN

8 WADDEN SEA COAST

The *Waddenzee*, or Wadden Sea, (Frisian: *Waadsee*, German: *Wattenmeer*, Danish: *Vadehavet*) is the inland sea between the Wadden Islands and the North Sea on one side, and the mainland of the Netherlands, Germany and Denmark on the other side. The area stretches out between Den Helder in the Netherlands and Esbjerg in Denmark, and has a length of 500km (310 miles) with an average width of 20km (12 miles). The surface area is approximately 10,000km² (6,200 miles²).

In the second half of the nineteenth century, many fishermen from Urk, Wieringen, Durgerdam, Huizen and Volendam fished in the North Sea directly north of the Wadden Islands. This was mainly done in

winter, because the fish they caught could then be kept alive in the bun for longer (see box, page 24) and kept cool with ice.

A number of major disasters at the turn of the nineteenth century drove many fishermen from that part of the North Sea and made them return to the Zuiderzee again. Moreover, there was quite a lot of competition with English fishermen, who also fished north of the Wadden Islands. Young boys who went out fishing earned so little money that they preferred signing up with the lugger fleets at Vlaardingen, IJmuiden and in Germany, where they could earn five times as much.

FRIESLAND WADDEN ISLANDS
TERSCHELLING

Many fishermen from the Frisian Wadden Islands signed up with herring luggers from Germany, IJmuiden or Vlaardingen because they could earn considerably more. To get there, they walked – mostly in groups – a distance of approximately 100–200km (62–124 miles). Initially, I thought that the fishermen on the Frisian Wadden Islands usually wore English machine-knitted sweaters, or almost identical home-knitted sweaters in stocking (stockinette) stitch with an Eye of God motif on the chest); however, new pictures have shown that they did wear more specific sweaters, with a variation of vertical bands.

103 THIS LUGGER FROM EMDEN, AE 101, COUNTED QUITE A FEW
TERSCHELLINGERS AMONG ITS CREW: GERRIT WORTEL, CORNELIS SCHOL, ANDRIES
ZORGDRAGER, GERRIT WEEVER, JETZE DE BEER, ALBERT WIEGMAN, DOUWE
KOOIJMAN AND EELKE DE BEER, CA. 1910. GEESJE LETTINGA, WEST-TERSCHELLING

TERSCHELLING 2 GANSEY

AGE: 10–11 YEARS (SIZE: 146CM/4FT 9½IN), CHEST CIRCUMFERENCE: 71CM (28IN) + 3CM (1¼IN) = 74CM (29¼IN), TOTAL HEIGHT: 56CM (22IN)

Knit a swatch first, with different sized needles if necessary. A gansey should not be too loosely knitted. Follow the chart for the motif and adjust the width and/or height to your size, the yarn used and your tension (gauge). Follow the general instructions for knitting ganseys on page 51 and adjust where necessary.

Measurements

WIDTH: 2 × 37cm (14½in) = 74cm (29¼in)

SHOULDERS: 11.5cm (4½in)

NECK: 14cm (5½in)

NECKLINE DEPTH: 3–4cm (1¼–1½in)

ARMHOLE HEIGHT: 17cm (6¾in)

HEIGHT UP TO ARMHOLE, EXCL. RIBBING: 33cm (13in)

SLEEVE LENGTH, EXCL. RIBBING: 38cm (15in)

WRIST CIRCUMFERENCE: approx. 20cm (8in)

RIBBING: 4–5cm (1½–2in), as preferred

Materials

∞ 9 balls SMC Merino Extrafine 120 in 0154 Jeans, or equivalent DK (light worsted/8-ply) yarn in jeans blue; 50g/131yd/120m

∞ 3mm (UK 11/US 2) and 3.5mm (UK 10/US 4) circular needles

∞ 3.5mm (UK 10/US 4) straight needles

∞ cable needle

TENSION (GAUGE): 23 sts × 30 rows in stocking (stockinette) stitch and 26 sts × 30 rows in cable motif on 3.5mm (UK 10/US 4) needles = 10 × 10cm (4 × 4in)

RIBBING: k1, p1

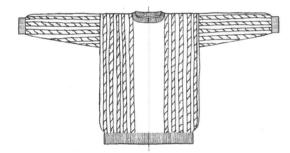

DETAIL OF BOY IN TERSCHELLING 2 GANSEY FROM FIG. 103, OPPOSITE

FRIESLAND
HARLINGEN/HET BILDT/ SINT JACOBIPAROCHIE

Harlingen has always been a bustling, busy city. From the seventeenth to the early twentieth centuries, it was an important industrial and seaport. For years, it was the third port in the Netherlands, after Amsterdam and Rotterdam. In 1920, the economy went into a downward spiral: companies went bust and production was moved elsewhere. After the Second World War, Harlingen recovered somewhat, and profited from the post-war reconstruction in the Netherlands. Fishing was an important economy booster, because after the completion of the Afsluitdijk dike in 1932, the city was the only Frisian seaport left. The fleet from Urk, for example, has sailed from the port of Harlingen since the Zuiderzee was cut off from the sea.

The two Harlingen ganseys found have horizontal bands with high-low tide motifs, or two alternate motifs.

104 UNLOADING AT THE MUNICIPAL FISH AUCTION AT THE HAVENPLEIN, CA. 1935. IN THE FOREGROUND, FISHERMEN FROM URK, WHO CHOSE HARLINGEN AS THEIR BASE OF OPERATIONS AFTER THE ZUIDERZEE WAS CLOSED OFF, BUSY ON THEIR SHIP, PUTTING FISH IN BASKETS. THE MEN IN CAPS ON THE QUAY LOOK ON WITH INTEREST. THE FISH AUCTION ON THE HAVENPLEIN WAS LOCATED HERE FROM 1932 TO 1953. HET HANNEMAHUIS, HARLINGEN

HARLINGEN 1 GANSEY

AGE: 11–12 YEARS (SIZE: 152CM/4FT 11¾IN), CHEST CIRCUMFERENCE: 76CM (30IN) + 4CM (1½IN) = 80CM (31½IN), TOTAL HEIGHT: 55CM (21¾IN)

Knit a swatch first, with different sized needles if necessary. A gansey should not be too loosely knitted. Follow the chart for the motif and adjust the width and/or height to your size, the yarn used and your tension (gauge). Follow the general instructions for knitting ganseys on page 51 and adjust where necessary.

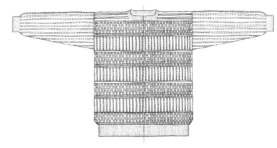

Measurements

WIDTH: 2 x 40cm (15¾in) = 80cm (31½in)

SHOULDERS: 13cm (5¼in)

NECK: 14cm (5½in)

NECKLINE DEPTH: 3–4cm (1¼–1½in)

ARMHOLE HEIGHT: 17cm (6¾in)

HEIGHT UP TO ARMHOLE, EXCL. RIBBING: approx. 34cm (13½in)

SLEEVE LENGTH, EXCL. RIBBING: 36cm (14¼in)

WRIST CIRCUMFERENCE: approx. 20cm (8in)

RIBBING: 3–5cm (1¼–2in), as preferred

Materials

∞ 10 balls Lang Thema Nuova in 0035, or equivalent 5-ply (sport) yarn in navy; 50g/129yd/118m

∞ 3mm (UK 11/US 2) and 3.5mm (UK 10/US 4) circular needles

∞ 3.5mm (UK 10/US 4) straight needles

TENSION (GAUGE): 23 sts x 34 rows on 3.5mm (UK 10/US 4) needles = 10 x 10cm (4 x 4in)

RIBBING: k1, p1

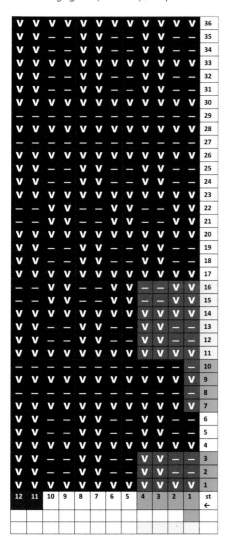

(Knitting chart, columns 12–1, rows 1–36)

105 A CARTE-DE-VISITE OF AN UNKNOWN BOY FROM AN ALBUM OWNED BY THE WIJGA-DROST FAMILY OF HARLINGEN, 1900–1910. THE BOY IS PROBABLY A FAMILY MEMBER OF EELKJE DROST OR HER HUSBAND HENDRIK WIJGA. HET HANNEMAHUIS, HARLINGEN

HARLINGEN 2 GANSEY

AGE: 12–13 YEARS (SIZE: 158CM/5FT 2¼IN), CHEST CIRCUMFERENCE: 80CM (31½IN) + 4CM (1½IN) = 84CM (33IN), TOTAL HEIGHT: 58CM (22¾IN)

Knit a swatch first, with different sized needles if necessary. A gansey should not be too loosely knitted. Follow the chart for the motif and adjust the width and/or height to your size, the yarn used and your tension (gauge). Follow the general instructions for knitting ganseys on page 51 and adjust where necessary.

Measurements

WIDTH: 2 × 42cm (18½in)= 84cm (33in)

SHOULDERS: 13.5cm (5¼in)

NECK: 15cm (6in)

NECKLINE DEPTH: 4–5cm (1½–2in)

ARMHOLE HEIGHT: 18cm (7in)

HEIGHT UP TO ARMHOLE, EXCL. RIBBING: 36cm (14¼in)

SLEEVE LENGTH, EXCL. RIBBING: 38cm (15in)

WRIST CIRCUMFERENCE: approx. 21cm (8¼in)

RIBBING: 4–5cm (1½–2in), as preferred

Materials

∞ 9 balls SMC Extra Soft Merino in 5402, or equivalent DK (light worsted/8-ply) yarn in navy; 50g/142yd/130m

∞ 2.5mm (UK 13/US 1) circular needles

∞ 2.5mm (UK 13/US 1) straight needles

TENSION (GAUGE): 23 sts × 34 rows on 2.5mm (UK 13/US 1) needles = 10 × 10cm (4 × 4in)

RIBBING: k2, p2

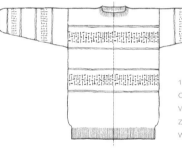

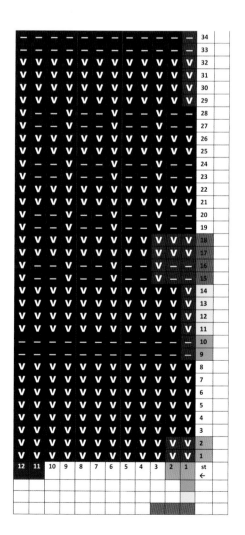

106 GERRIT VAN DER ZEE (BORN IN HARLINGEN ON 17/02/1895), WITH HIS FATHER BAUKE VAN DER ZEE AND BROTHER RIENTS VAN DER ZEE. THE GANSEYS WERE KNITTED BY THEIR WIFE AND MOTHER, AALTJE KUIKEN

In the autumn of 1893, the town of Wierum was going through bad times. Constant storms meant the fishermen could not leave the port to go fishing. At the end of November, the weather looked reasonable, and they decided to sail on December 1. After two and a half hours, they arrived at the first fishing ground. The weather turned bad that night, and they barely managed to get the first nets overboard. The catch was disappointing: only eighty fish. The wind, a south-easterly at first, turned towards the north. The sky clouded over. The first snowflakes arrived, changing to fine snow, and then turning into a snow storm. The wind turned easterly. The sea roared. The swell came from the southwest, against the storm. The ships were facing huge waves. Soon, the first ship went down, and others foundered on the beach of Ameland. Pieter Akkerman's ship managed to stay upright, and because the crew had tied themselves to the ship with the rigging they all stayed on board. Suddenly, Thys van den Bos's ship came right at them, threatening to hit them. That was the last thing they saw of the barge. Another ship followed later. There were only two left after that, theirs and Kris Kamma's, until that one went down too. Pieter stayed afloat. He was afraid of the Bornrif near Terschelling, a high and steep sandy ridge with a channel. Hitting that would shipwreck them. But again, a miracle happened. They were pulled through the channel and came out behind the islands, where it was safe. A few more ships from Wierum had made it there, worried about the others. He had to tell them that a lot of their family members had died. When Akkerman took off his sou'wester, he got a huge shock. All his hair had fallen out. He was completely bald, and his hair would never grow back. His black beard had turned snow white. Because in this small community everyone was related to everyone by marriage, not many houses were spared loss and pain.

www.jan.vanhemert.name

After 1800, fishermen living along the dikes in the north of Friesland started fishing on the Wadden Sea, which proved not to be very profitable. The fisherwomen had a very important role in both business and family: not only were they responsible for the household and the children, they also had to be good at baiting (putting fat sea worms, which they dug up at low tide, on hooks). The fishing grounds were soon depleted, and many ships were lost at sea in bad weather, causing the village to lose a large number of men.

The Wierum ganseys are very diverse, with both horizontal and vertical bands, filled with various motifs.

FRIESLAND
WIERUM

WIERUM 5 GANSEY

AGE: 13–14 YEARS (SIZE: 164CM/5FT 4½IN), CHEST CIRCUMFERENCE: 84CM (33IN) + 4CM (1½IN) = 88CM (34¾IN), TOTAL HEIGHT: 56–58CM (22–22¾IN)

Knit a swatch first, with different sized needles if necessary. A gansey should not be too loosely knitted. Follow the chart for the motif and adjust the width and/or height to your size, the yarn used and your tension (gauge). Follow the general instructions for knitting ganseys on page 51 and adjust where necessary.

Measurements

WIDTH: 2 × 44cm (17½in) = 88cm (34¾in)

SHOULDERS: 13.5cm (5¼in)

NECK: 14cm (5½in)

NECKLINE DEPTH: 4–5cm (1½–2in)

ARMHOLE HEIGHT: 18cm (7in)

HEIGHT UP TO ARMHOLE, EXCL. RIBBING:
    34cm (13½in)

SLEEVE LENGTH, EXCL. RIBBING: 34cm (13½in)

WRIST CIRCUMFERENCE: approx. 16cm (6¼in)

RIBBING: 4–6cm (1½–2¼in), as preferred

Materials

∞ 5 balls Scheepjes Zuiderzee in 3, or equivalent aran (worsted/10-ply) yarn in cream; 100g/218yd/199m

∞ 4mm (UK 8/US 6) and 4.5mm (UK 7/US 7) circular needles

∞ 4.5mm (UK 7/US 7) straight needles

∞ 3 buttons

TENSION (GAUGE): 19 sts × 24 rows on 4.5mm (UK 7/US 7) needles = 10 × 10cm (4 × 4in)

RIBBING: k2, p2

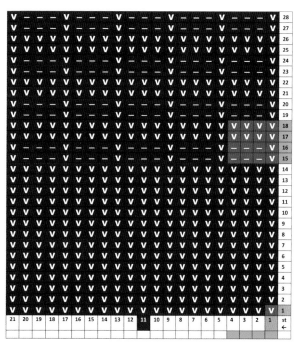

108 FISHERMAN'S MONUMENT ON THE DIKE NEAR WIERUM

FRIESLAND
PAESENS-MODDERGAT

Paesens-Moddergat, two towns so close together that they merged into one, is located in the far north of Friesland, close to the border with the province of Groningen. Many people know the town because of the terrible disaster of 1883, when in early March seventeen of the twenty-two ships that sailed out one morning were shipwrecked in a sudden storm. The majority of the male population was lost at sea. The town was shattered. The remaining ships were sold to towns in Zeeland and it took a long time before Paesens-Moddergat itself had a fleet again, now

moored in Lauwersoog. Many fishermen from this area signed on with the herring luggers of Vlaardingen, Emden and IJmuiden.

The Paesens-Moddergat 3 gansey, oppsite, is probably a copy of an English machine-knitted sweater from Cromer in Norfolk, on the English east coast, where luggers moored to take on water and salt. The gansey is definitely hand-knitted, as it has a cord with tassels woven through the collar. This was typical for Dutch ganseys. The ganseys from Paesens-Moddergat show various designs and motifs.

109 PAESENS-MODDERGAT, *WESTDONGERADEEL*, WL 19

110 YOUNG FISHERMAN FROM PAESENS-MODDERGAT, PHOTOGRAPHED IN HELLEVOETSLUIS, WEARING A GANSEY INSPIRED BY A SWEATER FROM CROMER, ENGLAND. MUSEUM 'T FISKERSHÚSKE, PAESENS-MODDERGAT

THE PAESENS-MODDERGAT 1, 2 AND 3 (CALLED ZOUTKAMP 2) AND 4 (NOW 3) GANSEYS CAN BE FOUND ON PAGES 127, 128 AND 131 OF *DUTCH TRADITIONAL GANSEYS*.

PAESENS-MODDERGAT 3 GANSEY

AGE: 10–11 YEARS (SIZE: 146CM / 4FT 9½IN), CHEST CIRCUMFERENCE: 71CM (28IN) + 3CM (1¼IN) = 74CM (29¼IN), TOTAL HEIGHT: 56CM (22IN)

Knit a swatch first, with different sized needles if necessary. A gansey should not be too loosely knitted. Follow the chart for the motif and adjust the width and/or height to your size, the yarn used and your tension (gauge). Follow the general instructions for knitting ganseys on page 51 and adjust where necessary.

Measurements

WIDTH: 2 x 37cm (14½in) = 74cm (29¼in)

SHOULDERS: 11.5cm (4½in)

NECK: 14cm (5½in)

NECKLINE DEPTH: 3–4cm (1¼–1½in)

ARMHOLE HEIGHT: 17cm (6¾in)

HEIGHT UP TO ARMHOLE, EXCL. RIBBING:
    33cm (13in)

SLEEVE LENGTH, EXCL. RIBBING: 38cm (15in)

WRIST CIRCUMFERENCE: approx. 20cm (8in)

RIBBING: 4–5cm (1½–2in), as preferred

Materials

∞ 7 balls SMC Merino Extrafine 120 in 0151 Royal, or equivalent DK (light worsted/8-ply) yarn in royal blue; 50g/131yd/120m

∞ 3mm (UK 11/US 2) and 3.5mm (UK 10/US 4) circular needles

∞ 3.5mm (UK 10/US 4) straight needles

∞ cable needle

TENSION (GAUGE): 22 sts x 36 rows on 3.5mm (UK 10/US 4) needles = 10 x 10cm (4 x 4in)

RIBBING: k2, p2

FISHERMEN FROM VOLENDAM, AROUND 1910. GWEN SEBUS

9 ZUIDERZEE COAST

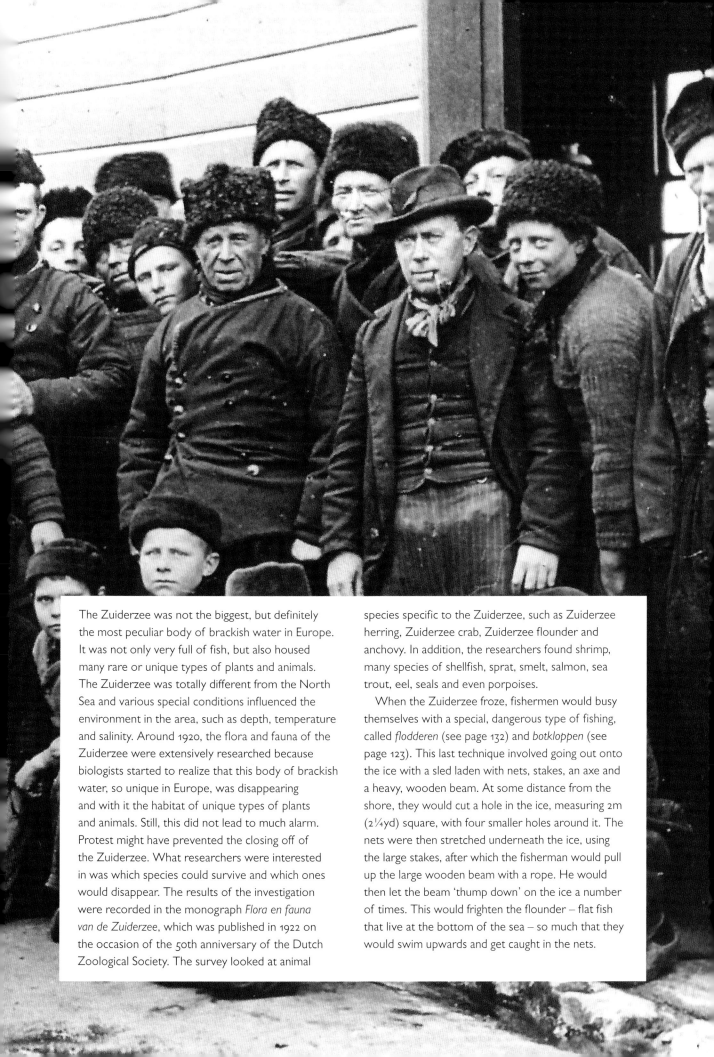

The Zuiderzee was not the biggest, but definitely the most peculiar body of brackish water in Europe. It was not only very full of fish, but also housed many rare or unique types of plants and animals. The Zuiderzee was totally different from the North Sea and various special conditions influenced the environment in the area, such as depth, temperature and salinity. Around 1920, the flora and fauna of the Zuiderzee were extensively researched because biologists started to realize that this body of brackish water, so unique in Europe, was disappearing and with it the habitat of unique types of plants and animals. Still, this did not lead to much alarm. Protest might have prevented the closing off of the Zuiderzee. What researchers were interested in was which species could survive and which ones would disappear. The results of the investigation were recorded in the monograph *Flora en fauna van de Zuiderzee*, which was published in 1922 on the occasion of the 50th anniversary of the Dutch Zoological Society. The survey looked at animal species specific to the Zuiderzee, such as Zuiderzee herring, Zuiderzee crab, Zuiderzee flounder and anchovy. In addition, the researchers found shrimp, many species of shellfish, sprat, smelt, salmon, sea trout, eel, seals and even porpoises.

When the Zuiderzee froze, fishermen would busy themselves with a special, dangerous type of fishing, called *flodderen* (see page 132) and *botkloppen* (see page 123). This last technique involved going out onto the ice with a sled laden with nets, stakes, an axe and a heavy, wooden beam. At some distance from the shore, they would cut a hole in the ice, measuring 2m (2¼yd) square, with four smaller holes around it. The nets were then stretched underneath the ice, using the large stakes, after which the fisherman would pull up the large wooden beam with a rope. He would then let the beam 'thump down' on the ice a number of times. This would frighten the flounder – flat fish that live at the bottom of the sea – so much that they would swim upwards and get caught in the nets.

NORTH HOLLAND
WERVERSHOOF/ MEDEMBLIK

The oldest city of West-Friesland is Medemblik, which was an important port on the western side of the Zuiderzee between Texel and Amsterdam in the seventeenth and eighteenth centuries. When the North Holland Canal was opened in 1824, and ships no longer needed to sail across the Zuiderzee to get to Amsterdam, the city lost its economic activity and even its harbour master. After 1887, fishermen from the area started to return to the port, to catch anchovy on the Zuiderzee. The fish auction was also restored.

Anchovy was a fish that required curing, and became more expensive with time. A lot of anchovy, called *sjoop* in the local dialect, was exported to Germany. The two salteries in Medemblik could hardly process the catch in 1890, so a third saltery was opened. The town also had a sailmaker and a cooper. On 1 January 1890, Medemblik had a population of 2,894, with fifty-eight fishing vessels and twenty-three turf ships.

Ganseys from Wervershoof/Medemblik are characterized by box motifs.

112 DORUS BERKHOUT AND SON (?) ON HIS *BOTTER*, WF 19, CA. 1949. OUD WERVERSHOOF

WERVERSHOOF 2 GANSEY

AGE: 10–11 YEARS (SIZE: 146CM/4FT 9½IN), CHEST CIRCUMFERENCE: 71CM (28IN) + 3CM (1¼IN) = 74CM (29¼IN), TOTAL HEIGHT: 56CM (22IN)

Knit a swatch first, with different sized needles if necessary. A gansey should not be too loosely knitted. Follow the chart for the motif and adjust the width and/or height to your size, the yarn used and your tension (gauge). Follow the general instructions for knitting ganseys on page 51 and adjust where necessary.

Measurements

WIDTH: 2 x 37cm (14½in) = 74cm (29¼in)

SHOULDERS: 11.5cm (4½in)

NECK: 14cm (5½in)

NECKLINE DEPTH: 3–4cm (1¼–1½in)

ARMHOLE HEIGHT: 17cm (6¾in)

HEIGHT UP TO ARMHOLE, EXCL. RIBBING: 33cm (13in)

SLEEVE LENGTH, EXCL. RIBBING: 38cm (15in)

WRIST CIRCUMFERENCE: approx. 20cm (8in)

RIBBING: 4–5cm (1½–2in), as preferred

Materials

∞ 6 balls Rowan Wool Cotton 4-ply in 487 Aqua, or equivalent 4-ply (fingering) yarn in baby blue; 50g/197yd/180m

∞ 2.5mm (UK 13/US 1) and 3mm (UK 11/US 2) circular needles

∞ 3mm (UK 11/US 2) straight needles

TENSION (GAUGE): 28 sts x 44 rows on 3mm (UK 11/ US 2) needles = 10 x 10cm (4 x 4in)

RIBBING: k1, p1

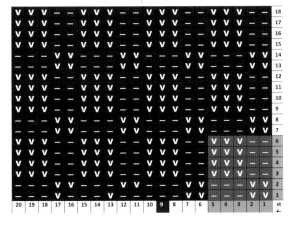

NORTH HOLLAND
VOLENDAM

In Volendam, ganseys (usually black) have been knitted for a long time and it is the only fishing town in the Netherlands where the gansey became part of the traditional costume. The Volendams Museum has a lot of ganseys with the characteristic high-low tide motif in horizontal bands, knitted in black sagathy. One is still on the needles, which shows you how thin they were for the yarn used (fig. 115). The high tide part of the motif consisted of variations of moss stitch, with the low tide in stocking (stockinette) stitch.

Volendam was the only Catholic fishing village in the Netherlands. The fishermen here fished with a *Volendammer kwak*, a type of barge. They fished on the Zuiderzee up to the North Sea, north of the Wadden Sea, catching anchovy, plaice, common dab and cod. In bad weather, the fishing vessels would take shelter in the ports of Terschelling and IJmuiden. The fishermen from Volendam were usually good at their work, but there were fishermen in all shapes and sizes: the 'golden fleet' comprised the one hundred best ships and fishermen. The 'wild chickens' were less-talented fishermen, and according to the villagers the 'sticklers' (*takkenleggers*) did not deserve to be called fishermen.

VOLENDAM 1 GANSEY

AGE: 12–13 YEARS (SIZE: 158CM/5FT 2½IN), CHEST CIRCUMFERENCE: 80CM (31½IN) + 4CM (1½IN) = 84CM (33IN) TOTAL HEIGHT: 58CM (22¾IN)

Knit a swatch first, with different sized needles if necessary. A gansey should not be too loosely knitted. Follow the chart for the motif and adjust the width and/or height to your size, the yarn used and your tension (gauge). Follow the general instructions for knitting ganseys on page 51 and adjust where necessary.

Measurements

WIDTH: 2 × 42CM (16½IN) = 84CM (33IN)

SHOULDERS: 13.5CM (5¼IN)

NECK: 15CM (6IN)

NECKLINE DEPTH: 4–5CM (1½–2IN)

ARMHOLE HEIGHT: 18CM (7IN)

HEIGHT UP TO ARMHOLE, EXCL. RIBBING:
36CM (14¼IN)

SLEEVE LENGTH, EXCL. RIBBING: 38CM (15IN)

WRIST CIRCUMFERENCE: approx. 21CM (8¼IN)

RIBBING: 4–5CM (1½–2IN), as preferred

Materials

∞ 11 balls Rowan Wool Cotton in 909 French Navy, or equivalent DK (light worsted/8-ply) yarn in dark navy; 50g/124yd/113m

∞ 2.5mm (UK 13/US 1) and 3mm (UK 11/US 2) circular needles

∞ 3mm (UK 11/US 2) straight needles

TENSION (GAUGE): 22 sts × 30 rows on 3mm (UK 11/US 2) needles = 10 × 10cm (4 × 4in)

RIBBING: k1, p1

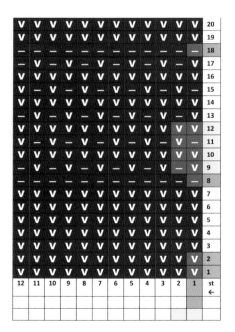

114 YOUNG FISHERMAN, CA. 1900. LAU SOMBROEK, VOLENDAM

VARIATION

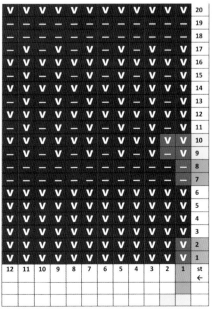

115 VOLENDAM GANSEY IN THE MAKING. VOLENDAMS MUSEUM

116 TWO BOYS FROM VOLENDAM, AROUND 1910.
LAU SOMBROEK, VOLENDAM

NORTH HOLLAND
DURGERDAM/ RANSDORP

Durgerdam, just north of Amsterdam, in Waterland, and now part of the municipality of Amsterdam, was a small fishing town on the Zuiderzee until it was closed off in 1932. It was part of Ransdorp and the fishing vessels sailed under the initials RD. When the Zuiderzee was closed off from the sea, this source of income largely disappeared. Most of the current inhabitants work in Amsterdam.

Miraculous rescue

On January 13, 1849, fisherman Jacob Bording, forty-five years old, and both his sons (Klaas, nineteen, and Jacob, seventeen) went out onto the ice of the Zuiderzee with a sled to go botkloppen (see page 117). In no time at all, they caught 750 fish and moved a bit further out to try again. The weather got bad, with thaw and rain, and they noticed that the ice was starting to break up and float. They tried to get home quickly, but a huge ice floe became detached from the shore, and they couldn't get back. They were stuck on the floe, and drifted on the Zuiderzee for fourteen days, in the most horrible conditions. They were frozen stiff, with feet swollen by the water. They collected rainwater in a piece of canvas and ate raw fish. Sometimes rescue seemed near, but every time they shouted out in vain. On Saturday morning, on 27 January, two small ships from the port of Vollenhove sailed along the wall of ice. They heard cries for help, and realized they must have found the fishermen from Durgerdam, whom they had heard about in Vollenhove. They called in the help of a flatboat and tjalk. The exhausted Durgerdammers were carefully transferred from the sled to the rowing boat. The floe and the sled immediately disappeared under water. Marretje, their wife and mother, arrived just in time to be with her eldest son Klaas when he died. Fourteen days later the father, Jacob also succumbed. A relief committee was immediately set up in Vollenhove, which raised enough money to provide the widow boarding with an annual allowance and to buy a fishing boat for the younger brother, Jacob.

www.henkvanheerde.nl

DURGERDAM GANSEY

AGE: 7–8 YEARS (SIZE: 128CM/4FT 2½IN), CHEST CIRCUMFERENCE: 62CM (24½IN) + 4CM (1½IN) =
66CM (26IN), TOTAL HEIGHT: 47CM (18½IN)

*Knit a swatch first, with different sized needles if necessary. A gansey should not be too loosely knitted. Follow the chart
for the motif and adjust the width and/or height to your size, the yarn used and your tension (gauge). Follow the general
instructions for knitting ganseys on page 51 and adjust where necessary.*

Measurements

WIDTH: 2 x 33cm (13) = 66cm (26in)

SHOULDERS: 10cm (4in)

NECK: 13cm (5¼in)

NECKLINE DEPTH: 3–4cm (1¼–1½in)

ARMHOLE HEIGHT: 15–16cm (6–6¼in)

HEIGHT UP TO ARMHOLE, EXCL. RIBBING: 30cm (11¾in)

SLEEVE LENGTH, EXCL. RIBBING: 32cm (12½in)

WRIST CIRCUMFERENCE: approx. 19cm (7½in)

RIBBING: 3–4cm (1¼–1½in), as preferred

Materials

∞ 6 balls Rowan Wool Cotton in 988 Larkspur,
  or equivalent DK (light worsted/8-ply) yarn in
  cerulean blue-green; 50g/124yd/113m

∞ 3mm (UK 11/US 2) and 3.5mm (UK 10/US 4)
  circular needles

∞ 3.5mm (UK 10/US 4) straight needles

∞ cable needle

TENSION (GAUGE): 21 sts x 28 rows on 3.5mm
(UK 10/US 4) needles = 10 x 10cm (4 x 4in)

RIBBING: k1, p1

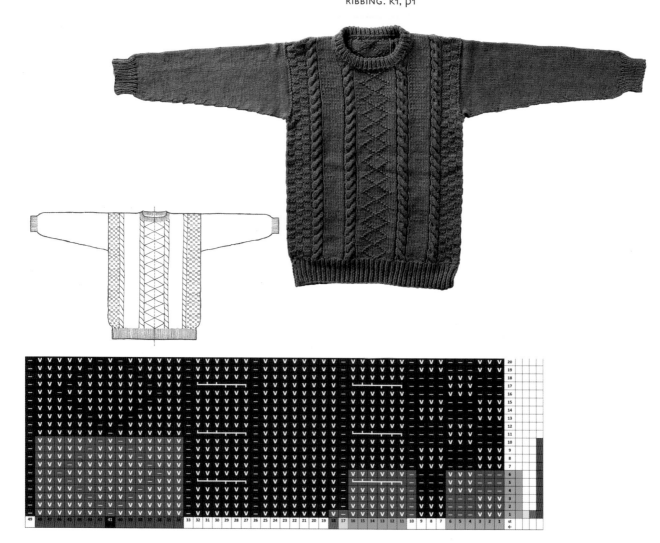

UTRECHT
BUNSCHOTEN-SPAKENBURG

The town of Spakenburg was situated on the Zuiderzee and had a port and a shipyard and merged with the neighbouring village of Bunschoten. As early as 1450, the Spakenburgers were selling their fish in Amersfoort. A century later, they had a fleet of eighteen or nineteen ships. The fleet blossomed between 1812 and 1892, growing from thrity-four to 193, as there were more markets where they could sell fish, both in the Netherlands and abroad. When the Zuiderzee was closed off from the sea after the completion of the Afsluitdijk dike in 1932, and the land was reclaimed

in the IJsselmeer, Spakenburg lost its importance as a fishing town. The processing of and trade in fish continued, but the fish was now brought in. To support the fishermen who had lost their jobs, a button factory was established in 1929, followed by a shoe and slipper factory in 1934.

The children's ganseys from Bunschoten-Spakenburg had a yoke, with horizontal bands on the body – this pattern differed from the adult ganseys, which alternated vertical bands of stocking (stockinette) stitch with bands of different cables.

BUNSCHOTEN-SPAKENBURG 4 GANSEY

AGE: 13–14 YEARS (SIZE: 164CM/5FT 4½IN),
CHEST CIRCUMFERENCE: 84CM (33IN) + 4CM (1½IN) = 88CM
(34¾IN), TOTAL HEIGHT: 56–58CM (22–22¾IN)

Knit a swatch first, with different sized needles if necessary. A gansey should not be too loosely knitted. Follow the chart for the motif and adjust the width and/or height to your size, the yarn used and your tension (gauge). Follow the general instructions for knitting ganseys on page 51 and adjust where necessary. Adjustments: the knitting order of the pattern in this gansey is reversed for the sleeves, to ensure that the patterns on the body and sleeves match when the gansey is worn. This means that the bottom-left wave pattern is knitted upside down. At the start of the cable pattern, one stitch was increased for each cable, to prevent the fabric from pulling in. These stitches were decreased again in the first garter stitch row/round.

Measurements

WIDTH: 2 × 44CM (17½IN) =
    88CM (34¾IN)

SHOULDERS: 13.5CM (5¼IN)

NECK: 14CM (5½IN)

NECKLINE DEPTH: 4–5CM (1½–2IN)

ARMHOLE HEIGHT: 18CM (7IN)

HEIGHT UP TO ARMHOLE, EXCL. RIBBING:
    34CM (13½IN)

SLEEVE LENGTH, EXCL. RIBBING: 34CM (13½IN)

WRIST CIRCUMFERENCE: approx. 16CM (6¼IN)

RIBBING: 4–6CM (1½–2¼IN), as preferred

Materials

∞ 12 balls Hjertegarn Vital in 6500,
    or equivalent DK (light worsted/
    8-ply) yarn in dark blue; 50g/126yd/115m

∞ 3mm (UK 11/US 2) and 3.5mm
    (UK 10/US 4) circular needles

∞ 3.5mm (UK 10/US 4) straight needles

∞ cable needle

TENSION (GAUGE): 20 sts × 28 rows on 3.5mm
(UK 10/US 4) needles = 10 × 10cm (4 × 4in)

RIBBING: k2, p2

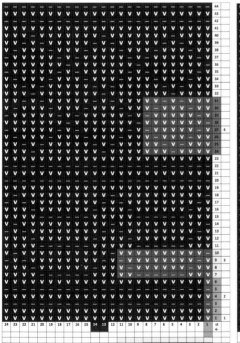

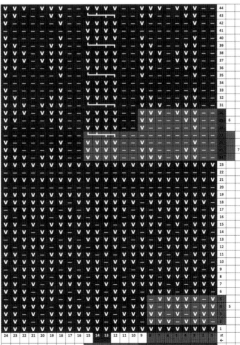

119 CHILDREN FROM SPAKENBURG
WEARING BUNSCHOTEN-SPAKENBURG
4 GANSEY, MEERTENS INSTITUTE
AMSTERDAM

BUNSCHOTEN-SPAKENBURG 6 GANSEY

AGE: 11–12 YEARS (SIZE: 152CM/4FT 11¾IN), CHEST CIRCUMFERENCE: 76CM (30IN) + 4CM (1½IN) = 80CM (31½IN), TOTAL HEIGHT: APPROX. 55CM (21¾IN)

Knit a swatch first, with different sized needles if necessary. A gansey should not be too loosely knitted. Follow the chart for the motif and adjust the width and/or height to your size, the yarn used and your tension (gauge). Follow the general instructions for knitting ganseys on page 51 and adjust where necessary.

Measurements

WIDTH: 2 x 40cm (15¾in) = 80cm (31½in)

SHOULDERS: 13cm (5¼in)

NECK: 14cm (5½in)

NECKLINE DEPTH: 3–4cm (1¼–1½in)

ARMHOLE HEIGHT: 17cm (6¾in)

HEIGHT UP TO ARMHOLE, EXCL. RIBBING:
approx. 34cm (13½in)

SLEEVE LENGTH, EXCL. RIBBING: 36cm (14¼in)

WRIST CIRCUMFERENCE: approx. 20cm (8in)

RIBBING: 3–5cm (1¼–2in), as preferred

Materials

∞ 8 balls Hjertegarn Mini Vital in 698, or equivalent 5-ply (sport) yarn in navy blue; 50g/164yd/150m

∞ 2.5mm (UK 13/US 1) and 3mm (UK 11/US 2) circular needles

∞ 3mm (UK 11/US 2) straight needles

∞ cable needle

TENSION (GAUGE): 26 sts x 32 rows on 3mm (UK 11/US 2) needles = 10 x 10cm (4 x 4in)

RIBBING: k1, p1

DETAIL OF BOY WITH THE BUNSCHOTEN-SPAKENBURG 6 GANSEY, FROM FIG. 118 ON PAGE 126

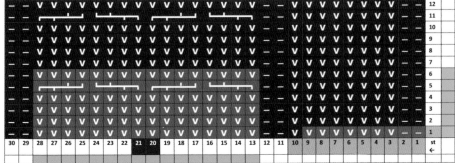

GELDERLAND
HARDERWIJK

Harderwijk was the most important fishing port on the east side of the Zuiderzee. Harderwijk had around 700 fishermen, who fished for Zuiderzee herring, flounder, smelt, common dab and anchovy. Their cured and smoked herring, known as Harderwieker, was very well-known and popular, both in the Netherlands and abroad. When the Zuiderzee dam and causeway was put into use in 1830, Harderwijk was no longer accessible for the ever-growing fishing vessels, as the port entrance was blocked by a huge sand bank. This problem was finally solved in 1925, but then the completion of the Afsluitdijk dike on 28 May 1932 was a huge blow for the fishing industry in the town. Harderwijk was

compensated somewhat by an expansion of the port. In 1967, the dike to the new province of Flevoland was completed, as a result of which Harderwijk became a city on a 'lake'. The fishing life of old is now getting the honour it deserves: the fish auction house, built in 1913 and later demolished, has been rebuilt; two new 'old' sheds with a recreational and educational functions were built in the old port; and the Harderwijker Botter Foundation now owns several of the 171 old HK barges – oak flat-bottomed fishing boats that once belonged to the fleet.

Various ganseys with a vertical design were found in Harderwijk, but also a number with a continuous motif that was worked all over the sweater.

120 PORT OF HARDERWIJK WITH *BOTTERS*, CA. 1910

121 FISHERMAN WITH BOY FROM HARDERWIJK, CA. 1950. CITY MUSEUM HARDERWIJK

HARDERWIJK 4 GANSEY

AGE: 1½–2 YEARS (SIZE: 92CM/3FT ¼IN), CHEST CIRCUMFERENCE: 56CM (22IN) + 4CM (1½IN) = 60CM (23½IN), TOTAL HEIGHT: 36CM (14¼IN)

Knit a swatch first, with different sized needles if necessary. A gansey should not be too loosely knitted. Follow the chart for the motif and adjust the width and/or height to your size, the yarn used and your tension (gauge). Follow the general instructions for knitting ganseys on page 51 and adjust where necessary.

Measurements

WIDTH: 2 x 30cm (11¾in) = 60cm (23½in)

SHOULDERS: 9cm (3½in)

NECK: 12cm (4¾in)

NECKLINE DEPTH: 3–4cm (1¼–1½in)

ARMHOLE HEIGHT: 13cm (5¼in)

HEIGHT UP TO ARMHOLE, EXCL. RIBBING: 22cm (8¾in)

SLEEVE LENGTH, EXCL. RIBBING: 23cm (9in)

WRIST CIRCUMFERENCE: approx. 12cm (4¾in)

RIBBING: 3–4cm (1¼–1½in), as preferred

Materials

∞ 5 balls Lang Thema Nuova in 0035, or equivalent 5-ply (sport) yarn in medium blue; 50g/129yd/118m

∞ 3mm (UK 11/US 2) and 3.25mm (UK 10/ US 3) circular needles

∞ 3.25mm (UK 10/US 3) straight needles

∞ 4 buttons

TENSION (GAUGE): 21.5 sts x 36 rows on 3.25mm (UK 10/US 3) needles = 10 x 10cm (4 x 4in)

RIBBING: k2, p2

DETAIL OF BOY IN HARDERWIJK 4 GANSEY FROM FIG. 121, OPPOSITE

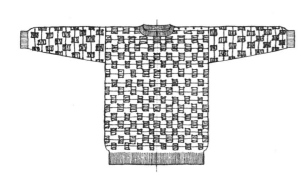

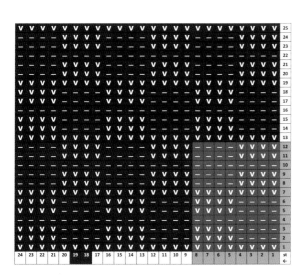

GELDERLAND
ELBURG

From early spring (February and March) until Easter, the fishermen from Elburg would fish for Zuiderzee herring in the same ways as the other fishermen on the Zuiderzee. They would use drift nets, which were pulled along in between two *botters*. Only a few vessels would use vertical nets. They would work with a crew of three on a barge. With this method, they could fish for flounder just off the coast, when the water was quiet and the wind was offshore. The fishermen did not earn much, and often relied on charity. To catch fish in the winter, they would go out onto the frozen Zuiderzee to go *flodderen*: after cutting a hole in the ice, they would insert vertical nets to catch smelt. It was a dangerous enterprise, because if ice floes broke off, they had no way of getting back to shore.

In Elburg, people did not remember that ganseys were ever worn. However, a number of them were found, all with a different design.

ELBURG 4 GANSEY

AGE: 7–8 YEARS (SIZE: 128CM/4FT 2½IN), CHEST CIRCUMFERENCE: 62CM (24½IN) + 4CM (1½IN) = 66CM (26IN), TOTAL HEIGHT: 47CM (18½IN)

Knit a swatch first, with different sized needles if necessary. A gansey should not be too loosely knitted. Follow the chart for the motif and adjust the width and/or height to your size, the yarn used and your tension (gauge). Follow the general instructions for knitting ganseys on page 51 and adjust where necessary.

Measurements

WIDTH: 2 x 33cm (13in) = 66cm (26in)

SHOULDERS: 10cm (4in)

NECK: 13cm (5¼in)

NECKLINE DEPTH: 3–4cm (1¼–1½in)

ARMHOLE HEIGHT: 15–16cm (6–6¼in)

HEIGHT UP TO ARMHOLE, EXCL. RIBBING: 30cm (11¾in)

SLEEVE LENGTH, EXCL. RIBBING: 32cm (12½in)

WRIST CIRCUMFERENCE: approx. 19cm (7½in)

RIBBING: 3–4cm (1¼–1½in), as preferred

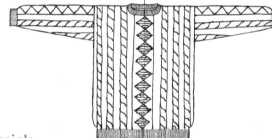

Materials

∞ 7 balls Rowan Wool Cotton in 983 Pier, or equivalent DK (light worsted/8-ply) yarn in baby blue; 50g/124yd/113m

∞ 3mm (UK 11/US 2) and 3.5mm (UK 10/US 4) circular needles

∞ 3.5mm (UK 10/US 4) straight needles

∞ cable needle

TENSION (GAUGE): 29 sts x 34 rows on 3.5mm (UK 10/US 4) needles = 10 x 10cm (4 x 4in)

RIBBING: k1, p1

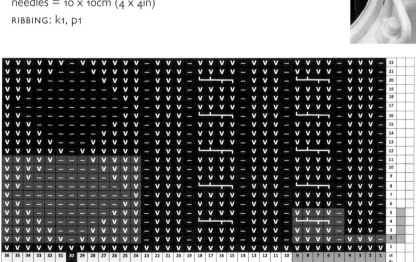

DETAIL OF BOY WEARING ELBURG 4 GANSEY, FROM FIG. 123, OPPOSITE

FLEVOLAND
URK

For a long time, agriculture was the main source of income on Urk, but the sea regularly destroyed the fields and crops. Many farmers turned to animal husbandry: butter from Urk was sold through the markets of Elburg and Kampen, and exported as far as Cologne.

In the sixteenth century the fishing industry grew, and more and more fishing vessels crossed the Zuiderzee north to go fishing in the North Sea. Amsterdam was an important market. Eventually, all grown men from Urk were working in the fishing industry. The fact that the industry continued after the Zuiderzee was closed off in 1932 is called 'the miracle of Urk'. When this happened the fleet moved to the port of Harlingen and sailed out to the North Sea, allowing the fish auction on Urk to continue to grow.

Urk was a very insular and isolated community, and the people there are a very proud and close-knit community to this day. Urk only got a connection to the mainland in 1939 because of the construction of dikes and land reclamation. This had enormous consequences for the people there. They had often intermarried, as they did in Marken, causing a higher risk of hereditary diseases. The very rare Van Buchem disease, which is characterized by excessive bone growth, resulting in paralysis and deafness, is common in Urk. The village is one of the most devout congregations in the Netherlands, they have their own dialect and even their own anthem.

The ganseys on Urk always use the same elements: the Eye of God, cables, Jacob's ladders and flags. The first three symbolize the closeness the Urker community felt to God.

126 FISHERMAN WITH HIS CHILDREN IN THE ANCHOVY SALTERY, CA. 1900. ZUIDERZEE CRAFT FOUNDATION, ENKHUIZEN

URK 1 GANSEY

AGE: 13–14 YEARS (SIZE: 164CM/5FT 4½IN), CHEST CIRCUMFERENCE: 84CM (33IN) + 4CM (1½IN) = 88CM (34¾IN), TOTAL HEIGHT: 56–58CM (22–22¾IN)

Knit a swatch first, with different sized needles if necessary. A gansey should not be too loosely knitted. Follow the chart for the motif and adjust the width and/or height to your size, the yarn used and your tension (gauge). Follow the general instructions for knitting ganseys on page 51 and adjust where necessary.

Measurements

WIDTH: 2 x 44cm (17½in) = 88cm (34¾in)

SHOULDERS: 13.5cm (5¼in)

NECK: 14cm (5½in)

NECKLINE DEPTH: 4–5cm (1½–2in)

ARMHOLE HEIGHT: 18cm (7in)

HEIGHT UP TO ARMHOLE, EXCL. RIBBING: 34cm (13½in)

SLEEVE LENGTH, EXCL. RIBBING: 34cm (13½in)

WRIST CIRCUMFERENCE: approx. 16cm (6¼in)

RIBBING: 4–6cm (1½–2¼in), as preferred

Materials

∞ 14 balls Scheepjes Nevada Super Noorsewol Extra in 1724, or equivalent DK (light worsted/8-ply) yarn in light navy; 50g/87yd/80m

∞ 3mm (UK 11/US 2) and 3.5mm (UK 10/ US 4) circular needles

∞ 3.5mm (UK 10/US 4) straight needles

∞ cable needle

TENSION (GAUGE): 21 sts x 32 rows on 3.5mm (UK 10/US 4) needles = 10 x 10cm (4 x 4in)

RIBBING: k1, p1

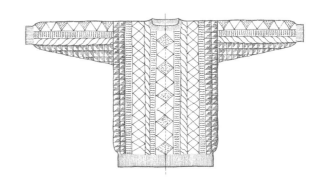

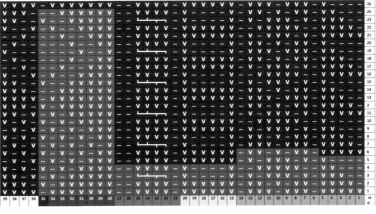

Two factors have contributed to the development of the fishing industry in Lemmer: the crisis in agriculture and the end of the peat industry in the south-east of Friesland. For peat workers, who often fished in inland waters to earn extra money, it was only a small step to start fishing on the Zuiderzee, as fishing still had plenty of opportunities for expansion at the end of the nineteenth century. A relatively small fishing vessel and a little bit of experience were enough to make good money. To buy the expensive nets, the local *hangbazen*, the fish smokers, would provide credit. This did mean that the fisherman had to sell his entire catch to the lender – who, quite unfairly, determined the price. The fleet was at its largest just after 1900, when fishing on the Zuiderzee suffered a major crisis. The population of Lemmer was largely non-religious

and the majority supported socialism; they were followers of Domela Nieuwenhuis, the first socialist in the Dutch Parliament. This meant the fishermen from Lemmer had no problems with working on Sundays. In 1894, the national Social Democratic Workers' Party was founded, and Lemmer got its local section shortly before 1900. In 1907, a more radical and Marxist movement split from the party, the Social Democratic Party, giving rise to the Communist Party for the Netherlands in 1918. This party also got a foothold in Lemmer, and found followers among the fishermen, especially the younger fishermen.

In Lemmer, people thought only machine-knitted English sweaters were worn, but home-knitted ganseys with various motifs have been found.

FRIESLAND
LEMMER

127 ANCHOVY CATCH IN THE PORT OF LEMMER, CA. 1900. ORIGIN UNKNOWN

LEMMER 2 GANSEY

AGE: 11–12 YEARS (SIZE: 152CM/4FT 11¾IN), CHEST CIRCUMFERENCE: 76CM (30IN) + 4CM (1½IN) = 80CM (31½IN), TOTAL HEIGHT: 55CM (21¾IN)

Knit a swatch first, with different sized needles if necessary. A gansey should not be too loosely knitted. Follow the chart for the motif and adjust the width and/or height to your size, the yarn used and your tension (gauge). Follow the general instructions for knitting ganseys on page 51 and adjust where necessary.

Measurements

WIDTH: 2 x 40CM (15¾IN) = 80CM (31½IN)

SHOULDERS: 13CM (5¼IN)

NECK: 14CM (5½IN)

NECKLINE DEPTH: 3–4CM (1¼–1½IN)

ARMHOLE HEIGHT: 17CM (6¾IN)

HEIGHT UP TO ARMHOLE, EXCL. RIBBING: approx. 34CM (13½IN)

SLEEVE LENGTH, EXCL. RIBBING: 36CM (14¼IN)

WRIST CIRCUMFERENCE: approx. 20CM (8IN)

RIBBING: 3–5CM (1¼–2IN), as preferred

Materials

- ∞ 7 balls Scheepjes Zuiderzee in 1, or equivalent aran (worsted/10-ply) yarn in dark navy; 100g/218yd/199m
- ∞ 3mm (UK 11/US 2) and 3.5mm (UK 10/US 4) circular needles
- ∞ 3.5mm (UK 10/US 4) straight needles
- ∞ cable needle

TENSION (GAUGE): 19 sts x 24 rows on 3.5mm (UK 10/ US 4) needles = 10 x 10cm (4 x 4in)

RIBBING: k1, p1

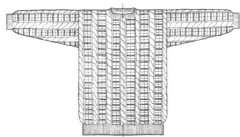

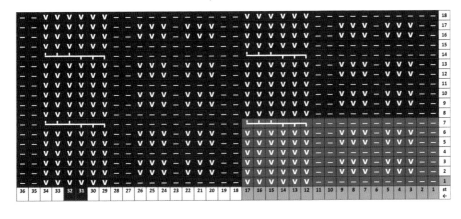

128 DETAIL OF BOY WEARING A HAND-KNITTED GANSEY

137

FRIESLAND
STAVOREN

In the Middles Ages, the herring would migrate to the Baltic Sea to spawn. Once fishermen learnt how to ensure they could extend the 'shelflife' of herring – by gutting and salting the fish – they would move to the the Sound strait en masse every summer. The fishermen came from Denmark and Germany, but also from cities in the Netherlands, such as Kampen and Stavoren. The Danish king allowed the fishermen to build huts on the shore near Skanör for the duration of the herring season. The men from Stavoren would build their own little village, called a *vitte*, which was governed by their own aldermen. This fishing industry came to an end when the herring migration changed direction after 1400. The herring would no longer swim towards the East Sea, but cross the North Sea towards the Channel. It heralded a period of decline. The situation improved slightly in the nineteenth century with the construction of the train track between Leeuwarden and Stavoren and the connecting ferry to Enkhuizen, both inaugurated in 1886, bringing a huge boost and economic growth. When the Afsluitdijk dam was built in 1932, the ferry became obsolete; however, it still runs in the summer season, and attracts a lot of tourists.

Three different ganseys were found in Stavoren.

129 THIS GROUP PHOTOGRAPH WAS TAKEN IN URK AROUND 1901/02, DURING THE HERRING SEASON. IT SHOWS FISHERMEN FROM STAVOREN AND FROM URK. IF THE HERRING SWAM FURTHER INTO THE BASIN OF THE ZUIDERZEE TO FIND ITS SPAWNING GROUNDS BEHIND URK AND ON THE KNAR NEAR HARDERWIJK, THE FISHERMEN WOULD FOLLOW THE HERRING FROM THE NORTH TO CATCH A PART OF THE SCHOOL. THE ORIGINAL PHOTOGRAPH IS OWNED BY BEREND BLEEKER FROM STAVOREN, BECAUSE IT SHOWS HIS GRANDFATHER

130 PORT OF STAVOREN, CA. 1900

STAVOREN 2 GANSEY

AGE: 12–13 YEARS (SIZE: 158CM/5FT 2¼IN), CHEST CIRCUMFERENCE: 80CM (31½IN) + 4CM (1½IN) = 84CM (33IN), TOTAL HEIGHT: 58CM (22¾IN)

Knit a swatch first, with different sized needles if necessary. A gansey should not be too loosely knitted. Follow the chart for the motif and adjust the width and/or height to your size, the yarn used and your tension (gauge). Follow the general instructions for knitting ganseys on page 51 and adjust where necessary.

Measurements

WIDTH: 2 x 42cm (16½in) = 84cm (33in)

SHOULDERS: 13.5cm (5¼in)

NECK: 15cm (6in)

NECKLINE DEPTH: 4–5cm (1½–2in)

ARMHOLE HEIGHT: 18cm (7in)

HEIGHT UP TO ARMHOLE, EXCL. RIBBING: 36cm (14¼in)

SLEEVE LENGTH, EXCL. RIBBING: 38cm (15in)

WRIST CIRCUMFERENCE: approx. 21cm (8¼in)

RIBBING: 4–5cm (1½–2in), as preferred

Materials

∞ 10 balls Rowan Pure Wool 4-ply in 455 Blue Iris, or equivalent 4-ply (fingering) yarn in cornflower blue; 50g/174yd/159m

∞ 2mm (UK 14/US 0) and 2.5mm (UK 13/US 1) circular needles

∞ 2.5mm (UK 13/US 1) straight needles

∞ cable needle

TENSION (GAUGE): 30 sts x 40 rows on 2.5mm (UK 13/US 1) needles = 10 x 10cm (4 x 4in)

RIBBING: k1, p1

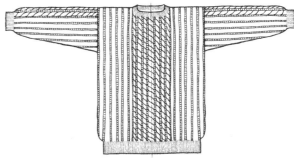

DETAIL OF BOY WEARING A GANSEY FROM STAVOREN. FROM FIG. 130, OPPOSITE

FRIESLAND
WORKUM

Workum, located approximately 12km (7½miles) south of Bolsward, on the Zuiderzee coast, is one of the smaller cities in Friesland. In the nineteenth century, Workum experienced growth because of the eel trade with London. Large volumes of eels were transported to London by eel barge, and unloaded on the shores of the Thames. When there was not enough domestically-caught eel available, eel would be imported from Denmark. Around 1900, the heyday of the eel came to an end. The last eel trader in Workum sold his business in 1907. The population did continue fishing for anchovy, but the number of actual fishermen was small. The captains from Workum also participated in the so-called 'Dung armada'. On *tjalken*

and *klippers*, they would sail 100 to 160 tonnes of cow manure from the south-west of Friesland to beyond the dunes at Warmond and Hillegom, where the soil was sandy.

The gansey in the photograph from Workum is difficult to see, but it shows a diamond-like motif, which has been used in this design.

132 FISHERMEN FROM WORKUM TRANSFER THEIR CATCH FROM THE *KAAR* INTO BASKETS, 1932. HIEKE AARDEMA, FRYSKE GROUN

131 FISHERMEN FROM WORKUM. HIEKE AARDEMA, FRYSKE GROUN

WORKUM GANSEY

AGE: 1–2 YEARS (92CM/3FT ¼IN), CHEST CIRCUMFERENCE: 52CM (20½IN) + 4CM (1½IN) = 56CM (22IN), TOTAL HEIGHT: 34–36CM (13½–14¼IN)

Knit a swatch first, with different sized needles if necessary. A gansey should not be too loosely knitted. Follow the chart for the motif and adjust the width and/or height to your size, the yarn used and your tension (gauge). Follow the general instructions for knitting ganseys on page 51 and adjust where necessary.

Measurements

WIDTH: 2 x 28CM (11IN) = 56cm (22in)

SHOULDERS: 8.5cm (3¼in)

NECK: 11cm (4¼in)

NECKLINE DEPTH: 3–4cm (1¼–1½in)

ARMHOLE HEIGHT: 11–12cm (4¼–4¾in)

HEIGHT UP TO ARMHOLE, EXCL. RIBBING: 18cm (7in)

SLEEVE LENGTH, EXCL. RIBBING: 21cm (8¼in)

WRIST CIRCUMFERENCE: approx. 12cm (4¾in)

RIBBING: 3–4cm (1¼–1½in), as preferred

Materials

∞ 3 balls Scheepjes Noorse Sokkenwol in 6861, or equivalent 5-ply (sport) yarn in natural; 100g/175yd/160m

∞ 2mm (UK 14/US 0) and 2.5mm (UK 13/US 1) circular needles

∞ 2.5mm (UK 13/US 1) straight needles

∞ 4 buttons

TENSION (GAUGE): 27 sts x 45 rows on 2.5mm (UK 13/US 1) needles = 10 x 10cm (4 x 4in)

RIBBING: k1, p1

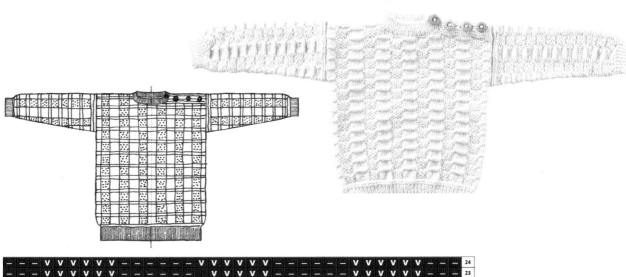

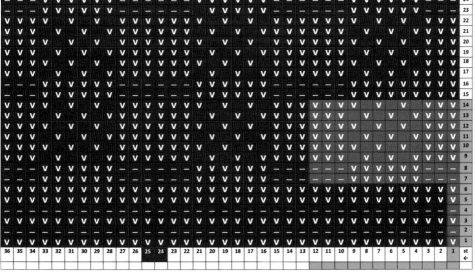

WORD OF THANKS

I do not have enough words to thank all the museums, historical societies, archives, private individuals, yarn suppliers and knitters for their time, effort and expertise, and for the material (pictures and otherwise) they made available to me. Without their help, this book could not be written. I would like to say a special thank you to Kees van der Plas and Jan van Beelen of the Katwijks Museum, Jan van de Voort and Alex Poldervaart of Museum Vlaardingen, Jacco Hooikammer of the Dutch Open Air Museum in Arnhem, Erik Walsmit of the Zuiderzee Museum in Enkhuizen, Peter Zuydgeest and Joke van Leeuwen-Zuidgeest of the Vlaardingen City Archives, Ihno Dragt of the Museum Dokkum and Museum 't Fiskershúske in Paesens-Moddergat, Mrs. Noordervliet-Jol of Muzee Scheveningen, Maarten Roeper of Museum Kaap Skil in Oudeschild and Berend Zwart of the Zoutkamp Fishing Museum, who shared their knowledge of fishing, customs and traditions, and the circumstances and working conditions in the period described – all at no cost. Of course, I am very grateful for all those other people, including Aaf Steur-Sombroek from Volendam, who provided me with beautiful photographs and sagathy, Mr and Mrs De Weert-Doesburg from Hippolytushoef, Fons Grasveld from Hilversum, Jeanine Otten of the Hannemahuis in Harlingen, Corien van der Meulen, Peter Overeem and Gertjan Baron of the City Museum in Harderwijk, Pieter Jan Klapwijk of the Maritime Museum in Rotterdam, Peter van Kooij and André Groeneveld of the Zuiderzee Museum in Enkhuizen, Gineke Arnolli of the Fries Museum, Maarten Noot of the KNRM in Den Helder, Jan Sander of De Egmonder Pinck, Janny Stecher-van den Berg of the Oudheidkamer Pernis, Jankees Goud from Yerseke, Chris Feij of the Arnemuiden Historical Association, Henk Klaassen of the Stichting Zuiderzee Craft Foundation in Enkhuizen, Henk de Jong from Willemstad, Joop Speulman of the Historical Archive of Charlois, Ton Mooijer of the Waterlands Archives in Purmerend, Arjens van Gammeren and Joop van Straten from Woudrichem, Willem van Norel of the Arent thoe Boecop Historical Association in Elburg, Piet Koomen of Oud Werfershoof in Werfershoof, Piet Morsch of the Zijper Archives in Schagerbrug, Ad Tramper of the Gemeentearchief Vlissingen, Piet Glas from Petten, Alexander de Bruin of the North Holland Archive in Haarlem, Reinder Storm and Jan Overduin from Vlaardingen, Jan Albregtse from Breskens, Carol Christiansen of the Shetland Museum in Lerwick, Shetland Islands, and William Moore from Scalloway, Shetland Islands, Deb Gillanders from Whitby, England, Job de Bondt of Scheepjes in Tynaarlo, Gerrit Brouwer and Erik van der Horst from Wilnis, Bianca Nagel of Handwerkzaak het Spoeltje in Almere-Haven, Saskia Piferoen of Lang Yarns in Korschenbroich, Germany, Jan and Russ Stanland of Farangipani Guernsey Wool in Penzance, England, Jo An Luijken of Wolhalla in Ruurlo, who published the Call for Knitters on their website, Trix de Waal from Ee, and Teuni Levering from Eelde.

I also want to warmly thank all the knitters, who were so enthusiastic about these patterns and who again achieved great results, the wholesalers who provided the materials for the ganseys, our models Ollie, Abel, Indra, Lotte, Daniel, Mees, Stef, Timo and Boaz and the moms and grandmothers who helped during the photo shoots by Gerhard Witteveen, Sietske Boonstra who edited the book, Ingrid van Roekel and Margo Togni of Studio Jan de Boer, who created a beautiful layout for this book, my husband, family and friends, who have supported me through thick and thin, and last but not least, Els Neele and the team at Forte, who worked their socks off to again produce such an amazing book.

If I have forgotten someone somewhere, please accept my warmest thanks!

CREDITS

Museums

Katwijks Museum,
Katwijk aan Zee
Kees van der Plas and Jan van
Beelen

Zuiderzee Museum /
Zuiderzeemuseum, Enkhuizen
Erik Walsmit, Peter van Kooij,
and André Groeneveld

Vlaardingen Museum /
Museum Vlaardingen,
Vlaardingen
Alexandra Poldervaart and
Dr. J.P. van de Voort

Muzee Scheveningen,
Scheveningen
Mevrouw Nel Noordervliet-Jol

Museum 't Fiskershúske,
Moddergat
Ihno Dragt and Trix de Waal

Dutch Open Air Museum /
Nederlands Openlucht-
museum, Arnhem
Jacco Hooikammer and
Hanneke van Zuthem

Museum Spakenburg,
Bunschoten/Spakenburg
Adriaantje de Jong

Fisheries Museum /
Visserijmuseum Zoutkamp,
Zoutkamp
Berend Zwart, Esther Toxopeus
and Truus Nienhuis

City Museum / Stadsmuseum
Harderwijk, Harderwijk
Corien van der Meulen and
Peter Overeem

Museum Het Oude Raadhuis,
Urk
Mevrouw A. Woord-Ras

National Sea Rescue Museum
/ Nationaal Reddingmuseum
Dorus Rijkers, Den Helder
Henk Stapel

Het Hannemahuis, Harlingen
Jeanine Otten

Fries Museum, Leeuwarden
Gineke Arnolli

Museum Noordwijk
Noordwijk Historical Society /
Genootschap Oud Noordwijk
Sjaan en Eli van Kekeren-Brouwer

Maritime Museum /
Maritiem Museum, Rotterdam
Pieter-Jan Klapwijk and Patricia
Mensinga

Fisheries Museum /
Visserijmuseum Aike van Sien,
West-Terschelling
Aike en Geesje Lettinga

Toankamer 't Ponthús, Stavoren
Andries Visser and Jan Visser

Museum het Arsenaal,
Woudrichem
Joop van Straaten

Shetland Museum, Lerwick,
Shetland Islands
Carol Christiansen

Scalloway Museum, Scalloway,
Shetland Islands
William Moore

The Mo, Sheringham Museum,
Sheringham, Norfolk, England
Philip Miles

Propagansey, Whitby,
Yorkshire, England
Deb Gillanders

Archives and societies

Meertens Instituut (KNAW),
Amsterdam
Diedrik van der Wal and Tineke
Tegelaers

City Archive /
Stadsarchief Vlaardingen
Joke van Leeuwen-Zuidgeest
and Peter Zuydgeest

North Holland Archive /
Noord-Hollands Archief,
Haarlem
Alexander de Bruin

KNRM Archive /
Archief KNRM, Den Helder
Maarten Noot

Historical Archive /
Historisch Archief Arnemuiden
Chris Feij

Municipal Archive /
Gemeentearchief Vlissingen
Ad Tramper

Streekarchief Goeree-
Overflakkee
Jan Both

Bomschuitclub, Zandvoort
Rob Bossink

Oudheidkamer Pernis
Janny Stecher-van den Berg

Historisch Egmond
Louis van der Zeijden, Martijn
Mulder and Harry Harms

Zuiderzee Craft Foundation /
Stichting Zuiderzeeambachten,
Enkhuizen
Henk Klaassen

Historical Archive of /
Historisch Archief Charlois,
Rotterdam
Joop Speulman

Municipal Archive /
Stadsarchief Gemeente
Amsterdam

Municipal Archive /
Gemeentearchief Den Haag

Wool wholesalers

Scheepjes, Tynaarlo
Job de Bondt

G. Brouwer, Wilnis
Gerrit Brouwer and Erik van
der Horst

Lang Yarns, Switzerland
Saskia Piferoen

Hjertegarn, Denmark
Craft store 't Spoeltje, Almere
Bianca Nagel

Frangipani Guernsey Wool,
England
Jan en Russ Stanland, Penzance,
Cornwall
www.guernseywool.co.uk

Knitted Knots, Rolde
Riek Siertsema
www.knittedknots.nl

De Noordkroon, Texel
Renske v.d. Tempel

Coats, Duitsland

Foula Wool
Magnus
www.foulawool.co.uk

Jamieson's of Shetland
www.jamiesonsofshetland.co.uk

Jamieson & Smith
www.shetlandwoolbrokers.co.uk

Knitters

Alie van Schouwenburg, Raalte
Urk 1 Gansey

Anja de Groot, Drachten
Wervershoof 2 Gansey

Antoinette Hendriks, Houten
Vlaardingen 9 Gansey

Astrid Pereboom, Bloemendaal
Arnemuiden 1 Gansey

Bella Dekker, Rotterdam
Harderwijk 4 Gansey

Bianca Boonstra, Bleiswijk
Lemmer 2 Gansey

Dineke Woldhek, Wijhe
Colijnsplaat Gansey

Froukje Fokkinga, Amersfoort
Durgerdam Gansey

Gerdy Vrijhoef, Raalte
Spakenburg 4 and Terschelling
2 Ganseys

Greta Galama, Vries
Yerseke 5 and Bunschoten-
Spakenburg 6 Ganseys

Harma Boven, Musselkanaal
Zwartewaal 5 Gansey

Heleen Bierling, Groningen
Woudrichem 4 Gansey

Hennie Lubberdink, Deventer
Arnemuiden 5 Gansey

Hieke Pereboom, Jirnsum
Elburg 4 Gansey

Hilda van Dijk, Tzum
Zandvoort 3 and Egmond 5
Ganseys

Jacqueline Jansen, Alphen a/d Rijn
Woudrichem 3 Gansey

Jannie Gelling, Gieten
Wierum 5 Gansey

Jannie Woldhuis, Eelderwolde
Harlingen 1 Gansey

Jenny de Boer, Tolbert
Harlingen 2 Gansey

Kitty Neijssel, Groningen
Charlois Gansey

Lenie Tensen, Lambertschaag
Scheveningen 6 Gansey

Liesbeth Boekhorst,
Oosterbeek
Arnemuiden 2 Gansey

Marian Smolders, Assen
Paesens-Moddergat 3 Gansey

Marja van Hout, Haarlem
Vlaardingen 8 Gansey

Marthy van der Kamp, Buren
Yerseke 2 Gansey

Mirjam Korfage, Hoorn
Katwijk 2 Gansey

Nanette Drijfhout-de Graaff, Langbroek
Scheveningen 7 Gansey

Nienke Koedam-de Boer, Losser
Pernis 5 Gansey

Rennie Knoop, St Nicolaasga
Katwijk 6 and De Paal Ganseys

Saskia Klijnsma, Groningen
Pernis 4 and Stavoren Ganseys

Saskia Vogel, Duiven
Middelharnis 5 Gansey

Stella Ruhe, Amsterdam
Den Helder 7, Katwijk 7 and Workum
Ganseys

Trix de Waal, Ee
Volendam 1 Gansey

Will Tol-Krabbendam, Lemmer
Noordwijk Gansey

Literature

Jan T. Bremer, Nationaal Reddingmuseum
Dorus Rijkers & Historische Vereniging
Den Helder, 1998

*The Illustrated History of the Nineteenth
Century*, Simon Adams et. al.,
Grange Books, 2000

Dutch Etymological Dictionary, Van Dale

The Very Easy Guide to Cable Knitting, Lynne
Watterson, St. Martin's Griffin, 2010

Cable Knits from Nordic Lands, Ivar Asplund,
Search Press, 2019

Viking Knits & Ancient Ornaments, Elsebeth
Lavoid, Search Press, 2019

Norwegian Knitting Designs, Margaretha
Finseth, Search Press, 2019

Knitting in the Nordic Tradition, Vibeke Lind,
Dover Publications, 2014 (English edition)

Guernsey and Jersey Patterns, Gladys
Thompson, B.T. Batsford Ltd., London, 1955

*Patterns for Guernseys, Jerseys & Arans:
Fishermen's Sweaters from the British Isles*,
Gladys Thompson, Dover Publications, New
York, 1969-1979

Fishermen's Sweaters, Alice Starmore, Anaya
Publishers Ltd, London, 1993

Fishing for Ganseys, The Moray Firth Gansey
Project, Kathryn Logan, Moray Firth
Partnership, Great Glen House, Inverness

Cornish Guernseys & Knit-frocks, Mary Wright,
Ethnographica, London

Heirloom Knitting, Rita Taylor,
Search Press, London, 2013

Websites

www.isgeschiedenis.nl
www.houtenhuis.nl
www.anemoon.org
www.vishandelkoning.nl
www.jenneken.nl
www.members.tele2.nl
www.noordzee.nl
www.biesbosch.nu
www.vakbondshistorie.nl
www.ekklesia-evangeliekorps.com

www.cultuurwijzer.nl/nwc.
ederlandsscheepvaartmuseum/cultuurwijzer.
nl
www.mijnzuiderzee.nl
www.historischegmond.nl
arjaentje.blogspot.nl
www.allesoverscheveningen.nl
www.rotterdam.nl
www.henkvanheerde.nl
www.rug.nl
www.dbnl.org
www.geschiedenisvanvlaardingen.nl
www.geschiedenisvanzuidholland.nl
www.hetlnvloket.nl
www.texel.net
www.ijsselmeervissen.nl
www.kistemaker.nlwww.mijnzuiderzee.nl
www.westfriesgenootschap.nl
www.huizer-botters.nl
www.verhalen-van-arian-van-diermen.
blogspot.nl
www.visserijdag-harderwijk.nl
www.visafslagelburg.nl/visserijverleden
www.onderzoekoverijssel.nl/detail.php
www.goedopstreek.nl
www.spanvis.nl
www.jan.vanhemert.name
www.flickr.com
www.museumhindeloopen.nl
www.vakbondshistorie.nl
www.entoen.nu/kinderarbeid
www.cultuurwijs.nl
www.historiegaasterland.nl
www.nevepaling.nl
www.regionaalarchiefalkmaar.nl
www.oosterschelde-
museum.nl

Photo credits

Most of the photos have the source
mentioned, in some cases, the source is
unknown. We tried our best to trace all
the right holders. If you feel you have the
copyright to an image in this book, please
contact the Publisher.

FIRST PUBLISHED IN GREAT BRITAIN IN 2020
SEARCH PRESS LIMITED
WELLWOOD, NORTH FARM ROAD,
TUNBRIDGE WELLS, KENT TN2 3DR

ORIGINALLY PUBLISHED IN THE NETHERLANDS
IN 2016
© 2016 Forte Uitgevers BV, Postbus 684,
3740 AP Baarn

TEXT, ILLUSTRATIONS, SWEATER NAMES,
PATTERNS AND KNITTING DIAGRAMS © STELLA
RUHE, 2016

PHOTOGRAPHS BY GERHARD WITTEVEEN,
APELDOORN; MARIA NEELE, ROTTERDAM; AND
STELLA RUHE, AMSTERDAM.
COVER AND INTERIOR DESIGN: STUDIO JAN DE
BOER, AMSTERDAM.

ISBN: 978-1-78221-752-7

THE PUBLISHERS AND AUTHOR CAN ACCEPT
NO RESPONSIBILITY FOR ANY CONSEQUENCES
ARISING FROM THE INFORMATION, ADVICE OR
INSTRUCTIONS GIVEN IN THIS PUBLICATION.

READERS ARE PERMITTED TO REPRODUCE
ANY OF THE WORK IN THIS BOOK FOR THEIR
PERSONAL USE, OR FOR THE PURPOSE OF
SELLING FOR CHARITY, FREE OF CHARGE AND
WITHOUT THE PRIOR PERMISSION OF THE
PUBLISHERS. ANY USE OF THE WORK FOR
COMMERCIAL PURPOSES IS NOT PERMITTED
WITHOUT THE PRIOR PERMISSION OF THE
PUBLISHERS OR AUTHOR.

SUPPLIERS
IF YOU HAVE DIFFICULTY IN OBTAINING
ANY OF THE MATERIALS AND EQUIPMENT
MENTIONED IN THIS BOOK, THEN PLEASE VISIT
THE SEARCH PRESS WEBSITE FOR DETAILS OF
SUPPLIERS: WWW.SEARCHPRESS.COM

THE PROJECTS IN THIS BOOK HAVE BEEN
MADE USING METRIC MEASUREMENTS, AND
THE IMPERIAL EQUIVALENTS PROVIDED HAVE
BEEN CALCULATED FOLLOWING STANDARD
CONVERSION PRACTICES. THE IMPERIAL
MEASUREMENTS ARE OFTEN ROUNDED TO THE
NEAREST $\frac{1}{8}$IN FOR EASE OF USE EXCEPT IN RARE
CIRCUMSTANCES; HOWEVER, IF YOU NEED MORE
EXACT MEASUREMENTS, THERE ARE A NUMBER
OF EXCELLENT ONLINE CONVERTERS THAT
YOU CAN USE. ALWAYS USE EITHER METRIC OR
IMPERIAL MEASUREMENTS, NOT A COMBINATION
OF BOTH.

North Sea Coast

DEN HELDER 7

EGMOND 5

ZANDVOORT 3

NOORDWIJK

KATWIJK 2

KATWIJK 6

KATWIJK 07

SCHEVENINGEN 6

SCHEVENINGEN 7

PERNIS 4

PERNIS 5

VLAARDINGEN 8

VLAARDINGEN 9

ZWARTEWAAL 5

MIDDELHARNIS 5

COLIJNSPLAAT

YERSEKE 2

YERSEKE 5

ARNEMUIDEN 1

ARNEMUIDEN 2

ARNEMUIDEN 5

DE PAAL